Children's Storybook Guidance

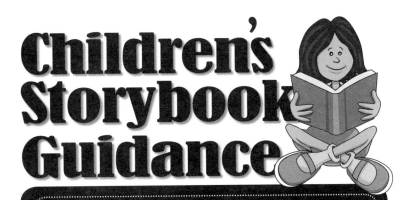

Inspirational Lessons and Activities Developed for 42 Counselor-Recommended Guidance Stories

youth light inc.

© 2012 by YouthLight, Inc. | Chapin, SC 29036

Layout and Design by Melody Taylor
Project Editing by Susan Bowman

Library of Congress Control Number
2012931288

ISBN
978-1-59850-115-5

10 9 8 7 6 5 4 3 2 1
Printed in the United States

Dedications

I would like to dedicate this book to my son J.C., his wife, Lindsey and my granddaughter, Cassadi. My son provided me with many opportunities to apply my counseling techniques and think outside the box. Family is the rock of any support network. Thanks for being there for me and always supporting and encouraging me.

Acknowledgments

Writing this book has taught me many things about myself especially the need to have a regular writing schedule. Without the ongoing support of my family and friends, this book would not have been possible. I would like to thank the following people:

To all my colleagues, past and present, that have influenced me, taught me and inspired me in so many ways, especially Becky and Cindy.

To my mentor, Bernie O'Connor who wore his heart on his sleeve. Your outlook on life, gentle ways, care and concern for others and openness to new ideas has impacted my life so much. As I wrote this book I could hear your words of encouragement as you watched from heaven

My colleague and friend, Sandy Ragona, who believed in me and encouraged me to write a book by myself! And especially for reviewing the book and providing valuable insights.

Bob and Susan Bowman for giving me the opportunity to write another book for their wonderful company. Also for being patient with me during this large undertaking.

Table of Contents

Focusing and Paying Attention

Friendship/ Empathy

Gossiping

Grief and Loss

Internet Safety/Personal Safety

Self Confidence and Motivation

The Secrets to Success

Appendix

Books with Multiple Guidance Topics

Introduction

As a parent or teacher, how can you use books to help children learn to stand up for themselves? To stand up for others? To express their feelings appropriately? To believe in themselves? To learn to pay attention at home and at school? To be able to cope with the divorce of their parents? Handle the loss of a beloved grandparent?

Books can be one way of helping children to recognize their own behavior and learn new behaviors. Books can take us to another place, stimulate our imagination and help us to realize that others have problems just like we do. They can

Books can be one way of helping children to recognize their own behavior and learn new behaviors.

provide comfort in knowing we are not the only ones experiencing this problem. Children will sit and listen to a story or pick up a book and "get lost" in it. Using books as a way to teach about difficult issues in their lives is what bibliotherapy is meant to do. As adults, we too, often look to books to help us find answers to problems in our own lives. We can provide the guidance for children to do this as well.

This book is intended to be used as a resource for parents, teachers, counselors or anyone working with children. The lessons can be used in a variety of settings – large group classroom, small groups, individual counseling or parents can read any of these resources with their children at home and discuss.

This resource is organized by concept. The chapters are broken down by concept areas and within each concept area are the books which discuss that topic. For each book, there is a general description of the book so you will know if it is appropriate for the child (ren) who will be using the resource. The materials and preparation needed to use the resource are included along with an introduction to the lesson, follow up questions and extension activities. There are some handouts or reproducibles which may be used with some of the lessons. I have tried to make the book as user friendly as possible.

Whatever your role with children, I hope this book will be a valuable resource that you will use for many years. Read on!

The History and Advantages of Bibliotherapy

Bibliotherapy is a unique type of therapy that has gained more recognition and attention over the past sixty years. The idea of healing through books is not new. Bibliotherapy can be traced back as far as the days when libraries first formed in ancient Greece (Aiex). However, it wasn't until the 1900's that the term, bibliotherapy, was used to imply the use of books as a therapeutic way to help people (Myracle, 1995) and not until 1946 that it was applied to children (Myracle).

Bibliotherapy has been defined many ways. As a way to treat through books (Pardeck, 1990), using books in a way that is "therapeutic in the sense that they can help children work through a crisis" (McCarty and Chalmers, 1997) and Hebert and Furner's (1997) definition as "the use of reading to produce affective change and to promote personality growth and development. It is an attempt to help young people understand themselves and cope with problems by providing literature relevant to their personal situations and developmental needs at appropriate times."

- **Three reasons outlined by Pardeck (1990) why bibliotherapy is effective when working with children are:**
  1. Children can obtain problem solving strategies through the experience of the characters in the book.
  2. Children can identify how the characters deal with similar anxieties, frustrations and disappointments that they may also be facing.
  3. Children gain insight into alternative solutions to the problems.

- **Children go through four stages when involved in bibliotherapy. They are:**
  1. Identification – the child identifies with a character in a book or story.
  2. Catharsis – the child becomes emotionally involved in the story and is able to release pent-up emotions under safe conditions – usually through discussion or activities.
  3. Insight – the child realizes their challenges can be overcome by understanding how the characters in the story solved their problems.
  4. Universalization – the realization that others have these problems as well.

A number of studies have been published showing the effectiveness of using bibliotherapy with children (Aiex, 1993; Forgan, 2002; Hebert & Furner, 1997; Kramer, 1999; Dramer & Smith, 1998; Myracle, 1995; Pardeck, 1990; Register et al., 1991; Salend & Moe, 1983; Schlichter & Burke, 1994; Schrank and Engels, 1981; Shechtman, 1999). Bibliotherapy has been shown to be very effective in helping children of divorce, being more assertive, changing attitudes, coping with disabilities and emotional problems, self-esteem issues; dealing with feelings and emotions, anxiety issues, motivation, values and morals, diversity, friendship, death and grief, teasing and bullying, anger and aggression, abuse, attention deficit hyperactivity disorder and illnesses.

Bibliotherapy is more than just reading a book. It is using a book in a way to teach, learn and heal. Bibliotherapy allows children to see their problems from a new perspective.

Bibliotherapy is inexpensive to implement. It is more than just reading a book. It is using a book in a way to teach, learn and heal. Bibliotherapy allows children to see their problems from a new perspective. It helps them realize that others have faced similar problems and solved them. Bibliotherapy offers strategies for children when they experience a similar problem or issue as a character in a book.

How to Implement Bibliotherapy

Implementing bibliotherapy is not difficult. It can be used in the classroom setting, small group setting, or in an individual counseling session. Parents can use the techniques at home to help with issues such as loss of a pet or death of a grandparent. The key is to find a topic that is appropriate for the class, small group or student and then find developmentally appropriate books that cover that topic. Be sure the book you choose is realistic. Does that mean animal stories aren't appropriate? Definitely not! As long as the animals in the story are ones the child will identify with and the problem is realistic, meaning it could happen in real life, it is a good choice.

Here are some steps to follow to ensure you're choosing a good book and have a plan to follow:

- Identify the child's needs. This can be done through observation, discussions with parents, student writing assignments or school records.

- Match the child with appropriate materials. Make sure the book is at the child's reading ability level, the text is interesting, the theme matches the child's need and the characters are believable so the child will empathize with their situations.

- Decide on a time and setting for the session.

- Motivate the child with introductory activities such as asking questions.

- Read the book to the child or if old enough, have the child read the book themselves.

- Ask questions to create discussion of the book, the problem, how it was solved, etc.

- Have follow up activities to reinforce the topics such as writing, puppets, drawing, etc.

- When appropriate let parents know what book(s) were read and the solutions that were discussed in the books.

Anger Management

There are many ways to express anger. Some are appropriate and others are not. While the kindergarten student may hit when someone tries to take their toys away, a fifth grade student may spread a rumor when someone won't let them sit by them at lunch. Reactions to anger may vary. The reaction can be physical, verbal or nonverbal. Counselors and teachers are often asked to work with students who express their anger in inappropriate ways.

The books in this section provide an opportunity for children to identify with characters that experience anger. The stories help children to understand it is okay to feel angry, it is how you express or react to the anger that may cause problems. Children will learn appropriate ways to handle anger, identify things that make them angry and learn some ways to cope when they are angry. These are valuable life skills.

Anger's Way Out

Book: *Anger's Way Out* by Karen Biron-Dekel

Publisher: Youthlight Inc.

Grade Levels: 4-8

Book Description: This is the story of Sam, a young girl who is a good athlete, has friends, is happy and has a nice family. She comes downstairs one morning expecting to talk about their upcoming vacation when her mom and dad tell her they aren't getting along. Sam knows what is coming – her parents are going to divorce. She experiences many different feelings. Sam has a hard time letting her anger out because she is afraid it will come out like her father's anger when he punched a hole in the wall. Sam learns how to appropriately handle her anger by talking with her school counselor. There are questions and activities at the end of the book.

Materials Needed: None

Preparation: None

Introduction: Ask students if they ever felt so angry they thought they might explode. What did they do with that anger? Tell them in the story you are about to read, Sam is afraid to express her anger so she stuffs it inside. Ask them to listen to find out what happens to Sam when she stuffs that anger and what she learns about anger.

Follow Up Questions

1. What feelings did Sam have when she found out her parents were getting a divorce?

2. Did she express those feelings? Why wouldn't she express her anger?

3. What happened to Sam's body as a result of not expressing her anger?

4. When you get angry where do you feel it?

Extension Activities

- Discuss with students some ways we physically feel anger (tension in our bodies, clenched fists, gritting teeth, etc.) Ask them if they can tell when they are getting angry before they express their anger. How can they tell? Do they know by the physical signs?

- Discuss with students some ways they may behave when they are angry (yelling, hitting, name calling, talking with someone they trust, etc.) Put these on the board. Have them tell which ones are hurtful to themselves or others. Ask them if they would be good choices? Brainstorm appropriate ways to behave and work through anger.

- Have students journal or draw about how they show emotions physically. Then have them write how they will appropriately express their anger at home and at school.

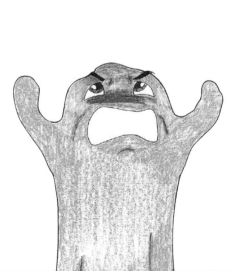

How Sam Learned to Express Her Angry Feelings in a Healthy Way

Out of This World

Book: *Out of This World: Face to Face with X-35* by Jon Filliti & Eric Erbes

Publisher: Youthlight Inc.

Grade Levels: 5-8

Book Description: In this comic book story, Max is transported to the Terrenia Universe. In order to get back home he helps the Unfortunates, a group who live in this universe who are being held captive by "The One." "The One" controls how much sun each planet receives so they are dependent on him. The Unfortunates are trying to get the catalyst from "The One" so they can be independent. While trying to get the catalyst they come upon X-35 who has anger issues. Max helps X-35 to understand it is okay to be angry but it is how you behave when you are angry that is important. Max teaches X-35 appropriate ways to control his anger. This book also includes activities that parents/teachers can use to help children learn to control their anger.

Materials Needed:
- Handout on Event, Feeling, Reaction
- Handout Appropriate/Inappropriate ways to handle anger

Preparation: Set up an anger control station in your classroom.

Introduction: Ask students if they ever get angry. Tell them you are going to read a story about a robot that gets angry. Ask them to listen for why the robot gets angry and what he does after he gets angry.

Follow up questions
1. How can you tell X-35 is angry?
2. The robot is being destructive. Have you ever acted this way when you were angry?

3. Can you tell when you are getting angry? How can you tell?

4. It's important to think about how you react when you get angry. What are some inappropriate ways to react? Appropriate ways to react?

5. Why is it important to work through anger in a controlled and appropriate way?

Extension Activities

■ Discuss with students that there is usually an event which triggers our anger and then we respond. Anger is okay. It is how we react when we're angry that is important. Have students make a list of inappropriate and appropriate ways to handle anger using the handouts.

■ Let students know there will be a anger control area in your classroom. In that area you can put squeezy balls, silly putty, thereaputty, an exercise ball they can sit on and bounce or move around, paper to write or draw about why they are angry, a CD player with quiet music and head phones, etc.

Activity 1

Write about events or situations that make you angry and how you react.

Event·····················▶ Feeling ·····················▶ Reaction

_____   _____   _____

_____   _____   _____

_____   _____   _____

_____   _____   _____

_____   _____   _____

★ List 3 ways you will respond next time you are angry or frustrated.

_____

_____

_____

_____

_____

Activity #2

Write Ways to Handle Angry Feelings

Inappropriate Ways	Appropriate Ways
______________________	______________________
______________________	______________________
______________________	______________________
______________________	______________________
______________________	______________________
______________________	______________________
______________________	______________________
______________________	______________________
______________________	______________________
______________________	______________________
______________________	______________________

Put a star next to the appropriate ways you will use to handle your anger.

Seemor's Flight to Freedom

Book: *Seemor's Flight to Freedom*
by Kimberly Nightingale and Nancy L. Walter

Publisher: Youthlight Inc.

Grade Levels: K-5

Book Description: Seemor is a sea gull who wears glasses. He loves to fly but has trouble landing smoothly. All the other sea gulls laugh at Seemor which makes him angry. One day he gets so angry when they laugh at him that he flies for three days and nights without stopping. He gets so tired he has to land. He hits the ground with a thud. He sees penguins standing around him and he waits for them to make fun of him. One penguin, Perceval, helps Seemor. The other penguins make fun of Perceval because he is so polite. The two birds walk off together. The book contains twelve lessons on how to control one's anger. Parents and teachers can help their children/students learn how to handle their anger by recognizing their feelings, the other person's feelings, who is "driving your taxi", empathy, and how to handle bullying.

Materials Needed:

- Thermometer with red for the temperature reading
- Pictures from magazines showing different feelings
- Handout on brainstorming anger
- Handout on what makes them angry

Preparation: Get white and red paper to make thermometers. Have students take out rulers, pencils and a black marker.

Introduction: During circle time, show your students some pictures and have them guess the feeling on each face. Ask them what feeling can get them into trouble. Have them show you their angry face. Ask them if they know when they are getting angry. Ask them what are some things that make them angry. Then share Seemor's story with them. Each time Seemor gets angry, make the temperature in the thermometer go up. At the end of the story, ask the students what the thermometer's temperature is.

Follow up questions

1. Why did the temperature go up?

2. What were some of the things that happened in the story to make Seemor angry and the temperature go up?

3. What did Seemor's face look like when he was angry? Do the activities in the book with the children.

Extension Activities

▪ Have the children make their own thermometers. Take some of the ideas they gave for why they get angry and use those to have the students show the level of anger with the thermometer by coloring the mercury red. For instance, when your brother/sister takes something of yours without asking how angry to you get? Show me on your thermometer – how angry it makes you.

▪ Have students write down the three things that make them most angry. Brainstorm with the children a list of ways to handle anger appropriately (listen to music, exercise, draw a picture, journal, etc.) Have students pick one way to handle each of the three things that make them most angry. Add on brainstorming handout.

▪ Have students pick an appropriate way to handle anger at home, on the playground, and in the classroom. Add on handout.

▪ Use a dry erase board to draw a thermometer and have different students respond to anger situations by coloring the level of anger on the thermometer.

Activity #3

How mad do you get in each situation? Write a number showing how mad you get.

1 = a little upset   2 = mad   3 = angry   4 = very angry   5 = explosive

Someone cuts in front of you in line: _____

Your best friend spreads a rumor about you: _____

You accidently spill juice on your new shirt: _____

Your little brother tears up your homework assignment: _____

Your friend is whispering something to another student about you: _____

You receive a mean text message about your best friend: _____

You find out that your friend lied to you about something: _____

Someone is sitting where you always sit in the cafeteria: _____

Choose 3 of the things that make you angry from the list above (3-5) and write an appropriate way to handle your anger for each one.

_____

_____

_____

_____

_____

Fill in the thermometer to show your level of anger for each situation.

Brother or sister comes in your room without asking.

A friend won't play with you at recess.

A friend says if you play with Tom / Mary they won't be your friend anymore.

Another student makes fun of you.

Brother or sister tells mom / dad you did something, but you really didn't.

Describe a recent situation

_____

_____

_____

Activity #5

[Ways I can Handle My Anger Appropriately]

Draw a picture or write ways you can handle your anger appropriately in the following settings:

 At Home

 On the Bus

 On the Playground

 On the Computer

 In the Classroom

 In the Cafeteria

Anxiety and Stress

The number of tests our students are required to take is increasing. They feel the pressure as early as second grade to do well on these tests. This pressure can lead to anxiety and stress. Stress and anxiety can also be experienced in home situations such as divorce, fighting among siblings, and the busy schedules that families have. The books in this section will provide some suggestions on how to handle stress and anxiety. Even as adults we have those times we need to take a moment, close our eyes and take a deep breath. It is important to teach children these strategies as well.

Miranda Peabody and the Stress-free Birthday Party

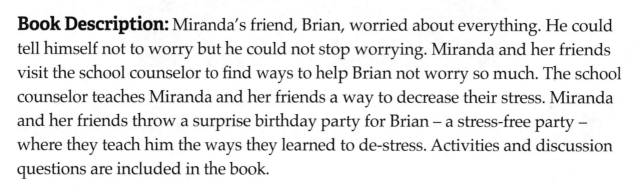

Book: *Miranda Peabody and the Stress-free Birthday Party*
by Susan DeBell

Publisher: Youthlight Inc.

Grade Levels: K-5

Book Description: Miranda's friend, Brian, worried about everything. He could tell himself not to worry but he could not stop worrying. Miranda and her friends visit the school counselor to find ways to help Brian not worry so much. The school counselor teaches Miranda and her friends a way to decrease their stress. Miranda and her friends throw a surprise birthday party for Brian – a stress-free party – where they teach him the ways they learned to de-stress. Activities and discussion questions are included in the book.

Materials Needed:

■ Poster for how to breathe

■ Handout on What works for me to calm down, de-stress, and not worry

■ Positive Self Talk Poster

Preparation: None

Introduction: Ask, "Have you ever worried about anything?" Ask students what they worry about. Then ask when they worry – just at bedtime, all day, etc. Tell them Brian Peterson worries a lot. He doesn't know how to make himself stop worrying. His friends are concerned about him. So concerned they want to help Brian learn to stop worrying. Listen to the story to find out ways anyone can stop worrying.

Follow up Questions

1. What was Brian worried about in the story?

2. Where did his friends go to get help for Brian?

3. What were some ways his friends learned they could stop worrying?

4. What is stress?

5. The children taught Brian what they learned about how to de-stress and stop worrying. Did it work for Brian?

6. Have any of you used these strategies to help you stop worrying?

7. Why do people worry? Does it solve the problem to worry?

Extension Activities

▪ Teach the children how to deep breathe. Tell them to inhale slowly through their nose to the count of four, hold it for four counts and slowly exhale through their mouths with their lips pursed and not making any noise to the count of four. Practice it numerous times with them. Give them a poster to hang in their classroom to remind them how to breathe.

▪ Teach them the strong sit.

▪ Have the children complete the handout, "Ways that work for me to calm down, de-stress and not worry."

▪ When feeling anxious, have the children look at the poster for Anxiety. Have children who worry or are perfectionists write on a card:

   I CAN do _____

   It is okay to make mistakes.

   I will try my best.

   If it isn't perfect the world will NOT end.

   Everything will be okay.

   Have them put the card on the corner of their desk or somewhere it is easily accessible.

   (Thanks to Sandy Ragona for sharing this great strategy with me a few years ago)

Activity #6

Things that I worry or get upset about

Things that will help me calm down and stop worrying

- When you are angry, frustrated or just need to calm down, follow these steps and BREATHE

- Breathe in slowly through your nose to the count of 4.

- Hold your breath for the count of 4.

- Slowly breathe out through your mouth to the count of 4. If you're doing it correctly, no one will be able to hear you breathing out.

- Do this as often as necessary to get CALM!

Positive Self-Talk

When I feel anxious, I will use positive self talk.

I can say:

It's okay to feel _____.

I can do this.

I can be calm.

Nothing horrible is going to happen.

The sky will stay up there.

Bullying and Teasing

A child goes home and says another child was picking on them at school. On the playground, a student takes the ball away from another student and won't give it back. What do you do? In the classroom, a student is whispering to another student. Most bullying takes place when adults are not around. How do we equip our children to handle these situations?

Books are a nonthreatening way to approach this topic and get conversation started. The books in this area have characters that are easy for children to relate to and are very realistic and believable. The characters in these stories use positive strategies to solve their problems with bullies. The bullies also learn lesson about how they appear to others. The strategies will empower children to stand up for themselves and to stand up for others.

Eliminating Bullying

Book: *Eliminating Bullying* by Sandy Ragona and Kerri Pentel

Publisher: Youthlight Inc.

Grade Levels: K-5

Book Description: This is a collection of stories for grades K-5 on how to handle bullying. The stories are about compassion, how to handle teasing, joking vs. bullying, ways to stand up for yourself and others, think before you act, and how to be assertive not passive or aggressive. Each lesson has a story, discussion questions, testimonials, activity sheets and a letter home to parents.

Materials Needed
- Handout: Teasing Situations

Preparation: None

Introduction: Choose the story that fits with the topic you want the children to learn. Follow the lesson plan for the story. Send the note home to parents.

Follow up Questions
I would use the follow up questions after each story. They are well written and applicable.

Extension Activities
- Use role playing to go along with some of the stories. For instance, with "The Teasing Game" give some examples of teasing that might happen on the playground and have the students practice using the four steps to handle teasing.

- When reading the "You Think It's Funny" story, have the students tell some jokes. Ask if the joke is funny or has it crossed the line to teasing. How do you know it has crossed the line? How do you know if it is appropriate?

How would you handle each of the following situations?

1. At lunch you go to sit down but the student sitting there puts their leg on the chair so you can't sit down.

   _____

   _____

2. At recess, someone makes fun of how you throw the ball.

   _____

   _____

3. An older student calls you "fatty."

   _____

   _____

4. You didn't do very well on the math test. Another student tells everyone what your score was. Then they say they were just kidding.

   _____

   _____

5. You fall down at recess and start to cry. The other kids call you a cry baby.

   _____

   _____

6. You saw a student take money from another student's locker. You report it to the teacher. The student calls you a tattletale and threatens to hurt you after school.

   _____

   _____

7. Make up your own situation and tell how you would handle it.

   _____

   _____

How to be a Bully! NOT!

Book: *How to be a Bully! NOT!* by Marcia Nass

Publisher: Youthlight Inc.

Grade Levels: 2-5

Book Description: Andy looks up to his big brother, Martin. Martin is cool and Andy wants to be just like him. Martin shows Andy the way to be cool is to be a bully. He teaches Andy three lessons about bullying. Andy discovers that good things happen to him when he treats others nicely. Martin ends up in trouble both at home and at school. There are activities at the end of the book to reinforce this message.

Materials Needed:
■ Handout on Advice for Younger students

Preparation: None

Introduction: Ask students if they know what a bully is. Ask, "Are bullies cool? "What makes a bully cool or not cool?" Tell them you are going to read a book about how to become a bully. Ask them to listen to find out what happens to the bully in the story.

Follow up Questions
1. Why does Andy want to be like his big brother?
2. How does Martin teach Andy to be "cool"?
3. What happens when Andy tries to bully other children?
4. At the end of the story, what happens to Martin?
5. What does it mean to be "cool?" Do you need to be a bully to be "cool"?

Extension Activities
■ What advice/suggestions would you give to someone who wants to be "cool?"
■ Have the students journal about the importance of being kind to others. What are the benefits of being kind? What are the drawbacks?

[Advice for Younger Students]

Pretend you are giving advice to younger students on how to not be a bully or to "be cool."

Advice #1

_____

_____

_____

Advice #2

_____

_____

_____

Advice #3

_____

_____

_____

Advice #4

_____

_____

_____

Kicky The Mean Chick

Book: *Kicky the Mean Chick* by Erika Karres

Publisher: Youthlight Inc.

Grade Levels: PK-2

Book Description: There are three stories in this book about Kicky the Mean Chick. In the first story, Kicky is mean to the other chicks and has to stand and watch the others play. She writes a letter of apology to the other chicks and they play with her again. In the second story, Kicky goes to kindergarten. The teacher, Ms. Schully, has to leave the room for a few minutes and tells the chicks to talk quietly but stay in their seats. A bully gets out of his seat and name calls and kicks the other chicks. When the teacher returns, Kicky stands up for those who were bullied and reports it to the teacher. In the last story, Kicky is so excited to be invited to a birthday party. When she gets there she encounters a chick clique who are making fun of how she looks. The other chicks come to her rescue and refuse to let the mean clique participate in the party. The children will enjoy the clever rhyming scheme in this book.

Materials Needed:
- Handout – Pledge to stand up for others
- Chick puppet (optional)

Preparation: None

Introduction: During story time, tell the children you will be reading a book that has three stories in it. The stories are about Kicky the Mean Chick. Ask what they think the story will be about. Ask them if anyone has ever been mean to them. Tell them to listen for how Kicky learns to be a nice chick.

Follow up Questions

1. What does Kicky do that is mean?

2. How do the other chicks feel when Kicky does and says these things?

3. What does Kicky have to do because she has been mean?

4. Is it important to stand up to a bully?

5. Why does Kicky tell the teacher about the mean chick in kindergarten?

6. Do you think Kicky was afraid the mean chick would be mean to her if she told?

7. What is a chick clique?

8. Who stopped the chick clique?

9. Do you have friends who would help you if you were being bullied by a clique?

Extension Activities

■ Talk about what to do when someone is being mean to you – ask them to stop, ignore it, walk away, or report to an adult. Based on your school's bullying program, talk about when to use each of these strategies.

■ Have the children draw a picture of a time when someone was mean to them. On the back side, have them draw how they would get the mean person to stop.

■ Have the students sign a pledge that says they will stand up for each other when someone is being mean.

Activity #9

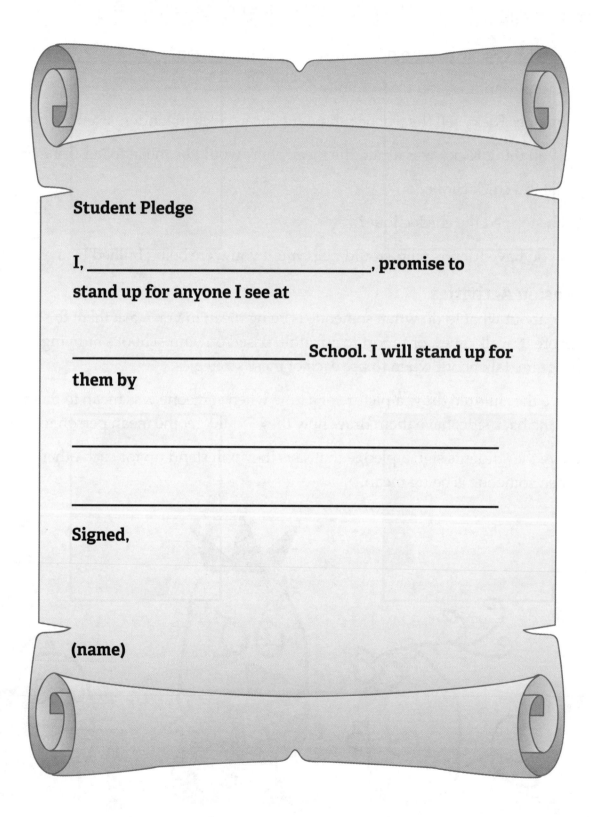

Student Pledge

I, _____, promise to stand up for anyone I see at

_____ School. I will stand up for them by

_____

_____

Signed,

(name)

Under each picture, write the feeling you see on the person's face.

_____

_____

_____

_____

Bully Victim Strategies

Unfortunately, bullying is a problem that needs to be addressed. It is found at school, in neighborhoods, at the park, on the Internet….basically it can be found anywhere. There is the victim, the bully and sometimes there are bystanders who watch or maybe even cheer on the bully. Parents, counselors and teachers need to empower children to handle bullies through education and support.

Teaching children how to handle bullies themselves empowers them to feel they can handle most situations without adult assistance. Sometimes when children tell an adult about a bully, the bullying increases. The stories in this section teach children strategies they can use to stand up to the bully before they go to an adult. Going to an adult needs to be a strategy that is used when they have tried other strategies on their own first. The stories in this section are about real situations that can and do happen to children so the children will easily identify with the characters. Just as we teach children what to do when a stranger approaches them, we need to give them the tools to know what to do when they are bullied or they see someone else get bullied.

How Not to be a Bully Target

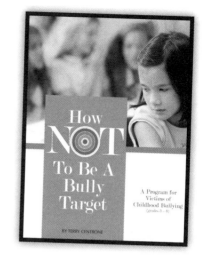

Book: *How Not to be a Bully Target* by Terry Centrone

Publisher: Youthlight Inc.

Grade Levels: 3-6

Book Description: This book contains ten stories about Mya, a girl who has just moved from Florida to New York. The stories tell how Mya is bullied by two girls in her fifth grade classroom. Mya learns how to stand up to bullies and be assertive. Each story comes with discussion questions, activities and handouts for students to learn about themselves and how to stand up to bullies.

Materials Needed:
- Poster board for victim, bully and bystander characteristics
- Poster board for how victims can be more assertive, how bystanders can help victims and how a bully can change their behavior
- Paper for a banner recognizing students who stand up to bullies

Preparation: None

Introduction: Tell the class that you will be discussing bullying. Ask them what it means and if they have ever experienced being bullied. Ask if they have ever seen someone else being bullied. You can read each story separately or use them together for a unit on bullying.

Extension Activities
- Discuss the roles of victim, bully, and bystander. Ask students to brainstorm characteristics of each role. Put these on a poster in your classroom.
- Talk with students about passive, assertive and aggressive behavior. Ask which goes with the role of victim, bully and bystander. Divide the class into groups. One group will make a list of ways a victim can learn to stand up for themselves. The second group will make a list of ways bystanders can help the

victim and stop bullies. The third group will make a list of things a bully can do to change their behavior and respond differently. Have students put their ideas on posters and decorate their posters to display in the classroom.

■ Have students make a banner. Every time a student stands up to a bully they will put the student(s) who stood up name(s) on the banner.

If You're Bothered and You Know It

Book: *If You're Bothered and You Know It* by Tricia Murin

Publisher: Youthlight Inc.

Grade Levels: K-2

Book Description: Tommy is an average looking kid who is not very athletic. Tommy learns how to stand up for himself when the kids call him names at the bus stop. He learns the difference between bullying and bothering when he has trouble focusing and taps his pencil on his desk during seatwork. There are five stories about Tommy in the book along with questions for discussion, activities and songs to remind students to do the right thing when being bothered or bullied.

Materials Needed: None

Preparation: None

Introduction: At the beginning of the school year, talk with students about the importance of standing up for yourself before going to an adult. Tell them you are going to read a story each day of the first week of school about Tommy and how he learned what to do when someone or something was bothering him or when someone was doing something he didn't like.

Follow up Questions

1. What did Tommy do when students called him a name at the bus stop?

2. Why didn't Tommy make fun of the students who called him a loser in football?

3. What is the difference between bothering and bullying?

4. What can you do if someone is bothering you or doing something you don't like?

5. What can you do if you see someone bothering or bullying someone else?

Extension Activities

■ Pair students up and have them practice saying "Please stop it." Name bullying/bothering situations that happen in the classroom, at recess, at lunch or on the bus.

■ Make sure the staff in your building who have recess and lunch duty know about "Please stop it." Make sure when a student reports bothering/bullying behavior to staff that he/she asks the student if they have asked the bully to stop first. If they have not, encourage the student to tell the bully to "Please stop it." Have the student role play it with you first. Be sure to have them look the bully in the eye and ask them to "Please stop it." If they have asked the bully to stop and the bully continues, then talk with the bully about appropriate behavior and have the bully write an apology to the student.

Book: *Please Stop I Don't Like That* by Sandy Ragona

Publisher: Youthlight Inc.

Grade Levels: K-5

Book Description: Joey and his friends are playing baseball. As can happen in a typical game on any school playground, there is name calling and making fun of others. Joey stands up and tells the bullies to "Please Stop I Don't Like That." He teaches his friends the importance of standing up for themselves and others. There are follow up activities at the end of the story.

Materials Needed: None

Preparation: None

Introduction: Tell students you are going to read a book about bullying on the playground. Ask them if they have ever witnessed bullying on the playground. Tell them the story will give them a way to stand up for themselves and others. Ask them to listen for how they can do that.

Follow up Questions

1. When the children went out to play kickball there was an argument about who got to pick teams. How did they solve the argument?

2. At the next recess, someone calls another child a mean name. How did Joey get Eli to stop calling him names?

3. The next day, they resume their kickball game. What did Mindy do when Jamal made fun of her? Was that a good choice? What would have been a better choice?

4. When Pablo says Amanda is out, does she argue with Pablo? What does she do?

5. What are the six magic words you can use to stop someone from doing or saying something you don't like?

Extension Activities

Talk with students about how important it is when you ask someone to stop to look them in the eye and with a calm but firm tone of voice ask the person to please stop I don't like that. Model this for the students. Pair students up and have one person play the part of a bully and the other be the person who will stand up for themselves. Give the students a typical bullying situation from the playground, lunchroom, bus or classroom. Have the bully do the bullying and the other student practice looking the bully in the eye and calmly but firmly saying please stop I don't like that. Then ask the student who was the bully if the other child looked them in the eye, used a calm but firm voice, and asked them to stop. Switch roles and continue to give situations to the students to practice.

Role Play Situations

- A student on the playground says you can't play ball with him/her and grabs the ball from you..

- You are standing in the lunchline at school when another student cuts in front of you.

- You are sitting in your usual place on the bus when an older student tells you to move because you are sitting in their seat.

- While in the classroom another student calls you a name as the teacher steps out of the room.

Out of This World – Tiglos vs. Secca Ma

Book: *Out of this World – Tiglos vs. Secca Ma*
by Jon Filitti and Eric Erbes

Publisher: Youthlight Inc.

Grade Levels: 3-8

Book Description: This is part 2 of the four part comic book series. This book continues where part 1 ended. Max and the Unfortunates have been captured by Secca Ma is who works for The One. They are taken to a place and held captive. Secca Ma takes Tiglo to a separate place from the others. It turns out at one time Tiglo and Secca Ma were friends but they separated when it became apparent to Tiglo that The One was trying to take over the world. Secca Ma tried to bully Tiglo into following The One but Tiglo refused and became his opposition. By working together Max and the others are able to escape their prison cell and leave that area. However, they must leave Tiglo behind. This comic book addresses why bullies bully, five steps to stop a bully and the importance of accepting our differences. It includes activities to reinforce the story.

Materials Needed: Deck of playing cards

Preparation: Take out the appropriate number of cards for the number of students in your class so you have fairly even numbers of the following groups: 2, 3 and 4; 5, 6, and 7; 8, 9, and 10; and Jack, Queen, and Kings.

Introduction: Ask the students to retell part 1 of the story. Ask them what they think will happen next. Read the story.

Follow up Questions

1. At one time, Tiglo and Secca Ma were friends. What happened to their friendship? Have you ever decided not to be friends with someone because you didn't like what they were saying or doing?

2. How did Max and the Unfortunates escape? Share a time when you worked together with others to accomplish something.

3. What is trust? Why is trust important in a friendship?

4. Name some ways you have used to try and stop a bully. Did they work for you?

5. If you were Max, would you have left your friend, Tiglo behind?

Extension Activities

■ Take a deck of cards and pull out enough Aces-Kings for your class. Try to have equal numbers of these groups of cards 2, 3, and 4's – the outcasts. Nobody wants to be around them. 5, 6, and 7's – the next to the lowest group. Only a few people will hang around them. 8, 9, and 10's – they are just below the popular group. Lots of people like to hang around with them. Jack, Queen and Kings- the popular group. Everyone wants to be with this group.

Tell the students you will be giving them each a card. They may not look at their card. They must put the card up to their forehead with the back of the card against their forehead. They will walk around the room. They must figure out what number is on their card by asking questions. Tell them about the above groups. Give an example. Put a card up to your head and walk around asking questions like – Let's play together at recess or Will you sit by me at lunch? Will you come to my birthday party? Tell them they must respond appropriately for the number the student has on their forehead. If I have a three they need to say no, walk away quickly, roll their eyes, tone of voice, etc. Put a sign up in different parts of the room for each group. Tell the students they must figure out as quickly as possible what group they belong to. When they know which group they are in, they must stand by the sign with the numbers of that group. Lay a card face down on each student's desk. Have them put the card to their forehead and walk around asking questions. Limit the time. After the activity, ask each group what it felt like to be in that group. Ask what the purpose of the activity was. Discuss how you as a class can prevent anyone from feeling unwanted. Sometimes, I will deliberately give bullies a 2, 3 or 4 so they can experience what it is like when no on wants them around and I give the least liked a Jack, Queen or a King to a student who is ignored and put down.

■ Have them write Part 3 of the story.

Bully Bystander Strategies

Bullies may be the children making fun of others or they can be the children who stand by and watch bullies making fun of others. If a child stands by and watches or laughs at what a bully is doing, they are just as much a bully because they are giving the bully permission to make fun of others. How do we get bystanders to take action? The books in this section give students strategies for ways to stop being a bystander and to help the victim of the bullying.

Becoming Someone's Hero

Book: *Becoming Someone's Hero* by Sandy Ragona

Publisher: Youthlight Inc.

Grade Levels: 2-5

Book Description: Joey and his friends are playing at recess when they see a bully yelling at another child. The group agrees quickly to go tell the bully to stop. Each person in the group says something to get the bully to stop. They then invite the victim to play with them. They all run off to continue their climbing game on the jungle gym leaving the bully by himself. The students talk about the five steps for bystanders to take to stop bullies instead of just standing around watching. The book includes activities, role play and writing ideas.

Materials Needed:

- Handout on friends you can go to and what words you would use to ask them for help

- Handout for drawing a picture of them with their friends standing up to a bully.

Preparation: None

Introduction: Ask students if they think there are more bullies or kids who aren't bullies in their class, school, neighborhood, etc. Ask them if there are times that others stand by and watch a bully be mean to another person. Tell them when someone stands by and watches a bully being mean to someone else they are just as guilty of bullying as the bully. By not doing anything, they are telling the bully that they agree with what he/she is doing. Tell them you are going to read them a story about bystanders. Ask them to listen for the five steps bystanders can take to stop a bully.

Follow up Questions

1. What did the students do when they saw Chase bullying Juan?

2. How did Juan feel when the other students came to his rescue?

3. Why did he call them heroes?

4. Would you have the courage to stand up for someone else?

5. How would you stand up for someone else even if the person being bullied is someone you don't like?

6. What were the five steps bystanders can take to stop a bully?

Extension Activities

- Use the handout to have students write the names of people they could go to if they were being bullied to ask them to go with them to stop a bully. Have them write what they would say to get the person to come with them to stop a bully next to each name.

- Ask students to think of a time when either they were being bullied or they saw someone else being bullied. Have them draw a picture showing them and their friends standing up to the bully.

Activity #11

Friends I Can go to for Help

Names of Friends I Can Ask To Help

_____

_____

_____

_____

_____

How I Would Ask Them to Help

_____

_____

_____

_____

_____

Either draw a picture or write a story showing you and your friends asking a Bully to stop.

Role play how you would go about getting the bully to stop.

Miranda Peabody and the Magnificent Friendship March

Book: *Miranda Peabody and the Magnificent Friendship March* by Susan DeBell

Publisher: Youthlight Inc.

Grade Levels: PK-4

Book Description: Miranda and her friends are looking forward to a new school year. As they stand on the playground, a new girl announces it is her playground and they better get out of there. The story is about bullying, bystanders and how to stop bullying. There are discussion questions along with activities to reinforce standing up to bullies at the end of the book.

Materials Needed:
■ Bullying survey

Preparation: None

Introduction: Ask the children if they know what a bully is. Then define it with their ideas and any additions that need to be made. Ask them if they know what bullying looks like. Tell them you are going to read a story about bullying. Ask them to listen for what the bully does, how the other students respond, and what was their solution to the bullying problem.

Follow up Questions

1. Who was the bully in the story? What did Maxie do to bully the other students?

2. How did they respond to Maxie's bullying?

3. Why didn't they tell the teacher?

4. Did the bullying stop when they followed their parents' advice?

5. What finally stopped the bullying?

6. Have you ever witnessed bullying at (name of your school)_____
   school?

7. Is there an anti- bully program or policy at your school? If so what is it? If not,
   what can you do to start one?

Extension Activities

■ Ask students to gather information about the types of bullying at their school.
   Have the children graph the types of bullying and then come up with a plan to
   stop it.

■ If there is an anti-bullying program or policy in the school, brainstorm with the
   children ways they can make sure everyone coming into the school knows what
   the program is and what to do if they encounter a bully.

■ Use the *Please Stop I Don't Like That* book and the *Becoming Someone's Hero* book
   for ways children can stop bullies and what bystanders need to do to stop
   bullies.

Bully Survey

[Understanding Harassment]

1. Have you ever been bullied or harassed at _____ school?   Yes   No

2. Have you ever seen anyone else bullied or harassed at _____ school?
   Yes   No

3. What type(s) of bullying or harassment have you seen or experienced:

   Verbal (name calling, put downs, threats, mean words, laughing at others, etc.)

   Physical (pushing, hitting, kicking, etc.)

   Nonverbal (eye rolling)

   Excludes others (won't let them play, sit by them at lunch)

   Is bossy, tells others what to do or not to do

   Won't let you play with others

   Spreads rumors

   Gossips

   Other _____

4. Where does the bullying take place most of the time?

   Class   lunch   hallway   bathroom   bus   playground   other _____

   Outside of school

5. When harassment problems occur do you first try to solve them yourself or go to an adult?

   Solve myself   Need an adult

6. What is harassment?

7. At what step of the Harassment Plan does the person being harassed write a letter to the person who is harassing them?   1   2   3   4

8. Is harassment against the law? Yes   No

Character

We hear a great deal about the lack of character and the rude way people act. We hear about the lack of citizenship and knowledge of what it means to be a good citizen. By learning to be people of character, it gives children a toolbox of ways to act, talk and behave that will be valuable to them throughout their lives.

Character involves the concepts of respect, responsibility, fairness, trustworthy, caring, and citizenship. Learning to treat others the way they want to be treated and using good manners is something children understand but sometimes have trouble doing. The books in this section model for children how to use these qualities in their lives. The importance of being a good citizen at school, in the community and in the world is emphasized.

Good Citizenship Counts

Book: *Good Citizenship Counts* by Linda D. Hagler

Publisher: Youthlight Inc.

Grade Levels: K-5

Book Description: This is a program to help children learn to be persons of character consisting of a leaders guide and ten story books. The first book is the teachers/parents guide. It gives a summary of each of the ten stories. After each summary is a list of anywhere from 7-12 activities which can be done to reinforce each of lesson topics. The topics include: *What is a good citizen? Why obey the rules? The Magic of Manner*s teaching children rules for good manners. *Grandpa's Knife* deals with the importance of respecting others property and suggestions for how to do it. *The Best Story Ever* tells about the need to be honest and not to cheat. *Everyone is special* teaches about how to accept the uniqueness and differences in others. *D.C.'s Adventure* challenges students to be responsible. *That's Mine! Keep Your Hands Off* explains the importance of sharing and taking turns. *Can I Help Save the World?* This book puts being a good citizen into action. It discusses ecology, where the food we eat comes from and the importance of taking care of our community, nation and world. *No Bath Tonight* emphasizes the importance of taking car of yourself through healthy eating, exercise, brushing your teeth and self-discipline.

Materials Needed:
- Handout Daily Self-Care Chart

Preparation: None

Have class vote on a project they would like to participate in which would benefit your community. Have them create a chart to keep track of who will do what for the project and how much you have done/collected.

Have students write announcements to be read daily during announcements about the project and why you are doing it. Include character traits in the announcements.

Introduction: Ask students what character is. Define it for them. Say each day or week for the next ten days or weeks, you will be sharing a story about how to be a person of character. Begin with the first story, *What is a Good Citizen Anyway?*

Follow up Questions

1. I would use the questions at the end of each book as they are well written and very applicable to each story.

Extension Activities

■ Using the handout, have children monitor how often each week they are taking care of themselves.

■ Set up a project your entire class or school can participate in to help someone in your community, volunteer for a community project or raise money, clothing, etc. for a community effort. Help them to understand the importance of helping people they do not know as well as helping those they do know. For instance, collect canned food for the local food pantry. Set a goal of how much you would like to collect. Chart how much has come in and how much you still need. Put the chart in the main lobby area of the school so everyone can see how much progress is being made. Send letters home to parents explaining what you are doing and why. Have the children write announcements to be read on the daily announcements to remind students about the canned goods and why you are collecting them. Include character traits such as citizenship, responsibility, and caring in the announcement.

Activity #13

[Daily Self-Care Chart]

For each day put an X in the box if you did that each day. If you did not do one of the items, leave the box blank. At the end of the week, check to see how you are doing with living a healthy lifestyle.

Day of the week	Bath or shower	Brush teeth	Comb hair	Healthy breakfast	Healthy Lunch	Healthy Dinner	Sleep 8 hours	Exercised
Monday								
Tuesday								
Wednesday								
Thursday								
Friday								
Saturday								
Sunday								

Families

The concept of a nuclear family is no longer the norm in our society. Children come from many different kinds of families. Some come from two parent families some from one parent families. Some live with grandparents, others live with foster families. Some have parents in jail. Some live in houses others in apartments. Some families have adults who work, others the adults cannot work. It is important for children to know whatever type of family they have, it is okay. No one type of family is better or worse than another.

We need to be careful of the words we use when describing families. Children of divorce get frustrated when adults refer to their home as "broken." They don't understand. To them their family is fine. It was "broken" when their parents lived together and fought a lot or never talked to each other. Children learn and repeat what they hear.

The books in this section help students to identify with different types of families. They promote acceptance of differences regardless of the type of family they have.

Who is in Your Family?

Book: *Who Is In Your Family?* by Susan Bowman

Publisher: Youthlight Inc.

Grade Levels: K-4

Book Description: There is no typical family. This book shares many different types of families by having a child from each family tell you about their own family. It is important for children to accept their families as they are and know that there is no "perfect" family. This book will help children with nontraditional families relate to one of the stories and feel free to talk about their family. There are discussion questions and activities that follow the story.

Materials Needed:
■ Handout on My Family Tree

Preparation: None

Introduction: Tell the children you want to learn more about their families. Ask them to tell you what a family is. Tell them the children in the story, *Who Is In Your Family?* come from different kinds of families. Ask them to listen for the family that is most like their own. Ask them also to listen for any families that are like their friends or relative's families.

Follow up Questions
1. Did you know there were so many different kinds of families?
2. Which family in the story is most like yours?
3. Have you ever met families like the others in the story?
4. Can you think of any families that weren't mentioned in the book?
5. Why is family important to you?

Extension Activities
■ Have students draw a picture of their family and write the names of the people (and animals) who are in the picture. Have the students share their pictures.

■ Have students bring in pictures of their family to share with the other students. Have them share things their family likes to do together.

[My Family Tree]

Draw a picture of your family starting with your parents in the center.

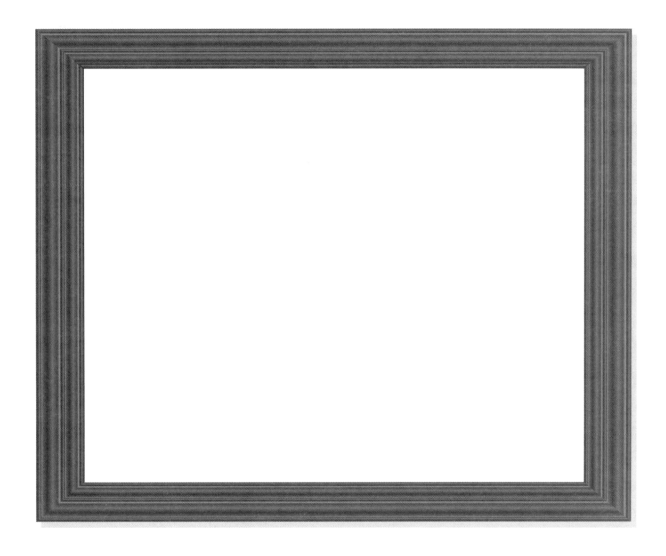

My Daddy is In Jail

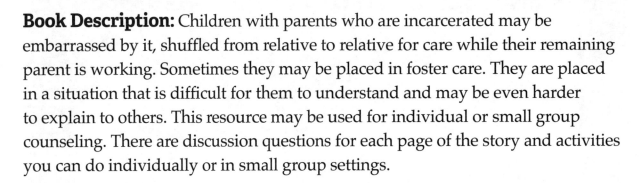

Book: *My Daddy is in Jail* by Janet M. Bender

Publisher: Youthlight Inc.

Grade Levels: K-5

Book Description: Children with parents who are incarcerated may be embarrassed by it, shuffled from relative to relative for care while their remaining parent is working. Sometimes they may be placed in foster care. They are placed in a situation that is difficult for them to understand and may be even harder to explain to others. This resource may be used for individual or small group counseling. There are discussion questions for each page of the story and activities you can do individually or in small group settings.

Materials Needed
■ Copies of the Who do you know who has been arrested or gone to jail? from the book

Preparation: None

Introduction: Tell the child(ren) you would like to share a story about a young girl whose father goes to jail. Have them do the Who Do you know who has been arrested or gone to jail sheet at the beginning of the book. If the children do not have a parent in jail, ask if they know of someone who is in jail.

Follow up Questions:
Use the questions in the book as they are written for the child to share what is happening in their lives and how it relates to the information on each page of the story.

Extension Activities
■ Give each child a notebook and let them decorate the front of it. It will be their own personal journal/diary. In the journal they can write any thoughts, feelings, worries, concerns, questions, etc. they may have between group meetings. Start off each group after the first meeting by asking if anyone has anything they have

written in their journal they would like to ask or share. Give them a journal they can take home and write in anytime they would like. Explain to the children that by writing down the things they worry about, wonder, are afraid of or just want to know helps to make them feel better. Tell them they don't have to share anything in the journal with anyone if they don't want to – it is for their personal use.

■ Use the handout to have the child(ren) draw a picture of what jail looks like to them. Have them write beneath it what they think happens to someone in jail.

Activity #15

Draw a picture of what a jail looks like to you.

What do you think happens when someone goes to jail?

_____

_____

_____

_____

Feelings

Everyone has feelings. All feelings are okay to have. It is how you express the feeling that is important. Children learn to express feelings from what is modeled for them. Teaching children how to handle their feelings in appropriate ways is something parents, counselors and teachers do on a daily basis. In order to handle feelings appropriately, children need to be able to identify the feeling first.

The books in this area, help children identify the feeling, accept the feeling and teach strategies for ways to express those feelings appropriately. The stories are very realistic and believable as are the characters.

Amigo, the Teardrop

Book: *Amigo, The Teardrop* by Betts H. Gatewood

Publisher: Youthlight Inc.

Grade Levels: K-5

Book Description: Can tears be helpful? Sometimes in our society, crying is frowned upon, especially for males. There can be an unspoken or spoken message that crying is for babies, sissies and children need to learn to handle situations without crying. The story of Amigo tells children it is okay to be sad and it is okay to cry. Crying helps us to feel better. The story explores times when children may be sad and how they can work through their sadness. Sometimes we can have tears of joy as well. The book contains questions for discussion of each new concept as well as activities for reinforcement of and identification with the concepts.

Materials Needed:
- Plain white paper, binder, cardstock, crayons or markers

Preparation: None

Introduction: Name some feelings you might have. When do you get sad? What do you do when you are sad? Today we will meet Amigo. Amigo is a teardrop. What's a teardrop? When might we have teardrops? Listen to find out ways you can help yourself feel better when you are sad.

Follow up Questions

1. We talked about what makes you sad. Were you surprised to hear some of the ideas to help yourself feel better? Which ideas surprised you? Which did you already know?

2. Is it okay to cry when you are sad?

3. Will or do others make fun of you when you cry? What do they say or do?

4. Explain that when you cry your brain releases endorphins – things which help us to feel better naturally. Is is okay to cry? Are there times you might want to cry by yourself? Are there times you want someone to be there when you cry? Who would you trust to be with you when you cry and not make fun of you?

5. Have you ever seen someone cry when they are laughing? Why do you think that happens?

Extension Activities

■ At circle time, have the children share times when they have been sad. Then have them tell what they did to feel better.

■ Have the children make a memory book of someone they loved who died. Have the child draw a picture of good memories they have of the person, favorite things they did with this person, etc. Then have them tell you about the memory. Type it on the computer and print it. Then keep it in a folder until all the memories have been drawn and written about. Put the sheets together and bind into a book. Have the child decorate the cover. This activity can be done in individual or small group counseling.

Ava Meets Amigo, the Teardrop

Book: *Ava Meets Amigo the Teardrop* by Betts H. Gatewood

Publisher: Youthlight Inc.

Grade Levels: K-5

Setting: Classroom, small group, individual, parents

Book Description: You met Amigo, the Teardrop earlier in this book. Now Ava meets Amigo when she is sad because her aunt is sick and in the hospital. Amigo helps Ava understand it is okay to cry when you are sad. Amigo also teaches Ava other ways she can help herself when she is sad.

Materials Needed: None

Preparation: None

Introduction: Talk about feelings. Ask students to name some feelings. Ask them where they feel their feelings – inside themselves. Ask, "Is it okay to feel mad? Sad? Happy? Afraid? Worried? Reinforce the idea that all feelings are okay. It is what you do with the feeling that can sometimes cause problems.

Ask the students if they have ever been sad. Then ask what happened that they felt sad. Tell them you are going to read a book about a girl who is sad. Ask them to find out how Ava can help herself feel better when she is sad.

Follow up Questions
1. Is it okay to be sad? What did Ava do when she was sad?

2. Is it okay to cry? How does crying help us feel better? (releases endorphins – chemicals that help us feel better)

3. What are some ways Amigo taught Ava to help her feel better?

Extension Activities
■ Using the handout, have students list ways they think will work for them when they are sad at home or at school.

■ Have students write in their journals ways they can help their friends when their friends are sad.

[Ways I Can Help Myself Feel Better When I Am Sad]

What are things you can do at home and at school when you are sad?

Things I Can Do At Home   **Things I Can Do At School**

_____   _____

_____   _____

_____   _____

_____   _____

_____   _____

_____   _____

_____   _____

_____   _____

Mustang, The Little Dog Who Was Afraid to go to School

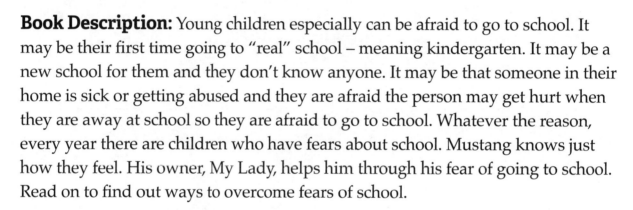

Book: *Mustang, The Little Dog Who Was Afraid to Go to School* by Jill Goodman

Publisher: Youthlight Inc.

Grade Levels: K-2

Book Description: Young children especially can be afraid to go to school. It may be their first time going to "real" school – meaning kindergarten. It may be a new school for them and they don't know anyone. It may be that someone in their home is sick or getting abused and they are afraid the person may get hurt when they are away at school so they are afraid to go to school. Whatever the reason, every year there are children who have fears about school. Mustang knows just how they feel. His owner, My Lady, helps him through his fear of going to school. Read on to find out ways to overcome fears of school.

Materials Needed: None

Preparation: None

Introduction: Ask the children, "What is fear?" If you have ever been afraid of something raise your hand. (Be sure you raise your own hand.) Have the children share what they were afraid of and share your fear as well. This way children know it is okay to be afraid – even adults have fear but you can't let your fear stop you. Tell them how you overcame your fear. Say some children are afraid of school. Mustang, the dog, knows just how they feel. Mustang is going to tell us how he overcame his fear of school. Listen for ways Mustang used to overcome his fear of school.

Follow up Questions

1. Why was Mustang afraid of school?

2. Have you ever been afraid of any of those things?

3. What did Mustang's owner tell him to do to help him overcome his fears?

4. Did it work?

Extension Activities

■ Talk with parents of any child afraid of coming to school at the beginning of the year. Have the parents make a plan with the child for something fun they will do when the parent gets home from work such as play a game, go for a bike ride, go to the park, read a special bedtime story, let the child choose the meal for dinner, etc.

■ Have the child meet with the school counselor to determine why the child is afraid to come to school. Is it they miss mom and/or dad? They are getting bullied. Then make a plan with the child that if they can go until morning recess without crying they can choose a friend to play a game, eat lunch with someone of their choice from school – their teacher, the counselor, a friend, etc.

■ Have a friendship group so the child can get to know other students and others can get to know the child.

■ Assign an older student to be his/her buddy.

Focusing and Paying Attention

Can you picture this? A student is looking out the window, another student has trouble paying attention when the teacher is talking, another is talking to others, and some are playing with things in their desk. These are some of the things that might interfere with students listening to the teacher and completing their work. Or it could be a child listening to their parents and doing their homework or chores. So how can you get your students/child(ren) to focus?

The books in this section offer practical solutions for parents, teachers, counselors and students. The characters are easy to identify with and the situations could happen in any classroom or home. The stories provide positive suggestions for ways to improve concentration.

Book: *Hocus Pocus Learn to Focus* by Randy Cazell

Publisher: Youthlight Inc.

Grade Levels: K-5

Setting: Classroom, small group, individual

Book Description: A student is looking out the window. Another student has trouble getting her work done when other students talk. Some students are talking during work time, playing with things in their desks, staring out the window, etc. These are just a few of the things that might interfere with students listening to the teacher and completing their work. This book addresses these issues and give students ideas for making a plan and finding ways to focus.

Materials Needed:
 3 x 5 index cards

Preparation: None

Introduction: Ask what it means to pay attention? How can you show someone you are paying attention? Today we will read, *Hocus Pocus Learn to Focus.* What do you think the story will be about? Let's see if you are right.

Follow up Questions

1. What problems did the students in Miss Lily Lioness' class have?

2. What does it mean to focus?

3. How did Brainy Butterfly help the students who had trouble focusing?

4. Can you think of any other strategies the animals could use to focus better in class?

5. Do any of you use strategies to help you stay focused? What are they?

Extension Activities

■ Give each student a 3 x 5 index card. Have them write three ways they personally need to focus.

■ As a teacher or parent, have a signal between you and the student/child which will be a reminder to them to focus. It can be a touch on the shoulder, the adult pulling their ear, etc.

Hunter and His Amazing Remote Control

Book: *Hunter and His Amazing Remote Control* by Lori Copeland

Publisher: Youthlight Inc.

Grade Levels: K-8

Setting: Classroom, small group, individual, parents

Book Description: Hunter is having a hard time paying attention. He has ADHD. While using the remote to turn off the television, Hunter thought that a remote might just help him. There are many useful buttons on a remote control that helped him to slow down and adjust his behavior so he could make better choices. The book includes a story about Hunter, activities explaining each button on a remote control and how they could help a child with ADHD as well as questions for discussion. Parents can read this book with their child and discuss each of the remote buttons and how it might help their child. Counselors can use this book in small group to help a child with ADHD manage their behavior. Classroom teachers can implement this book with the entire class.

Materials Needed:
- Heavy cardboard – like from a refrigerator box.
- Handout "Remote Control"

Preparation: None

Introduction: Today we're going to read the story of *Hunter and His Amazing Remote Control*. Listen for the unique way Hunter uses the remote control to help him in school and at home.

Follow up Questions
1. In what ways was Hunter a unique person?
2. Sometimes Hunter's gifts caused problems for him. Describe a problem Hunter had.

3. Why did others get frustrated with Hunter?

4. Why did Hunter make his own remote control?

5. What buttons did he put on his remote control? What did each button do?

6. Did the remote control help Hunter ? In what way?

Extension Activities

■ Children who have problems focusing can be helped by getting them to use both sides of their brain at once. Do the "pretzel" activity with the children when you notice they are losing focus. It can be done as a whole class or at home. Have the children hold their arms out in front of them with their hands facing each other. Then have them put one arm over the other arm. Now the backs of their hands are facing. Have them turn their hands so they face each other and clasp their hands together. Then have them pull their hands toward their chest and rest their hands on the chest. Then have them cross their feet and put their tongue on the roof of their mouth. Have them hold this position for two minutes. By crossing their arms and legs, they are crossing the midpoint of the body and engaging both sides of the brain. After doing this as a class, say anytime they find they are having trouble focusing at seatwork or when the teacher (parent) is talking they can make the pretzel. It doesn't disrupt the class and it will help the student to refocus.

■ Have the children make their own remote control and put the buttons on that they think will help them the most. Make the remotes out of heavy cardboard so they will last longer. Make the remote 3" x 7". You can use the model on the handout or make your own model.

[Remote Control]

Hey Max... Pay Attention The Importance of Concentration

Book: *Hey Max...Pay Attention! The Importance of Concentration* by Jon Filitti & Eric Erbes

Publisher: Youthlight Inc.

Grade Levels: 5-8

Setting: Small group, individual, parents

Book Description: This is Part 3 of the *Out of This World* series. Max and his friends escape Secca Ma but they have to leave Tiglo behind. They make a plan to save Tiglo. Max wants to help. He is given the job of watching the monitor. Max gets bored watching the monitor and misses an important message Tiglo is trying to send. The others get mad at Max. The comic book contains a leader's guide, questions for discussion, activities and suggestions for improving concentration.

Materials Needed: None

Preparation: None

Introduction: Do any of you ever have trouble concentrating when someone is talking or when you need to get something done? Part 3 of Out of This World is about those times when you have trouble concentrating and what you can do to pay attention. Listen to the suggestions for ways to improve your concentration.

Follow up Questions

1. When did Max lose focus?
2. How did Max feel when he realized he missed a communication from Tiglo?
3. How did the others react when they found out Max had missed communicating with Tiglo?
4. Most people have more trouble concentrating when they are sitting, are bored, or are doing routine activities. Do you have any other suggestions for ways Max could have focused better?
5. If you have trouble concentrating in school, who could you go to for help?

Extension Activities

- Use the handout in book to write about when you have trouble focusing and make a plan to improve your concentration.

- A technique Dr. Tom Ottavi taught me that is modified from Nancy Thomas', *When Love is Not Enough*, is called the Strong Sit. This technique needs to be practiced when the child is calm NOT during difficult times.

  - Have the child sit in a chair with both feet on the floor or cross-legged on the carpet.

  - Legs or feet are lightly pressed to the ground.

  - Hands are on the knees and lightly pressing down or folded in their lap.

  - Give them a spot on the wall to look at so they are not distracted and can really focus.

  - Breathe deeply and slowly.

  - Keep quiet and focus on the strength of feeling under control.

  - Start with very short periods of time and gradually increase the amount of time.

  - Be sure to reinforce the child for success and effort.

- Suggest that students play a game with you. They must sit very still. They cannot move any part of their body except to blink their eyes. Do this several times per day. See if they can increase the amount of time they can sit still. Chart their progress so they can see they are able to sit and focus for longer periods of time. This is can be done as a whole class but may work better in small group or individual counseling sessions.

Friendship/ Empathy

Regardless of age friendships are important to our well being. Friends provide the support system we need to encourage us when times are tough, to listen to us, play with us and accept us as we are. Learning how to be a good friend can be different at different stages of life. In the primary school years it is people who will play with us and like to do the same things we like to do. In the intermediate years of elementary school it is about friends we can trust with our secrets and our most intimate thoughts. During middle and high school years, peers become very important as a source of support, information, socializing and entering into intimate relationships.

Friendships have their ups and downs. To be a good friend takes work, being a good listener, keeping promises, using nice words and being an encourager. These stories share insights into friendship.

Shyanne

Book: *Shyanne* by Susan Bowman

Publisher: Youthlight Inc.

Grade Levels: K-5

Book Description: Shyanne is very shy just as her name implies. She is going to her second new school and she is too shy to say her name or ask someone to sit by her at lunch. The other children make fun of her. She visits with the school counselor who helps her learn ways to speak up through the use of puppets and other strategies. Overcoming shyness can be difficult for children. The book provides good techniques, activities and discussion questions.

Materials Needed
■ Handout – Ways I Can Make A New Student Feel Welcome in our Class/School

Preparation: None

Introduction: Tell the children you are going to read a book called *Shyanne*. Ask the children what they think the book will be about. Ask them what it means to be shy. Ask if they were ever shy or if they know someone who is shy. Ask them to listen for ways to help themselves and/or their friends overcome their shyness.

Follow up Questions
1. Why did the other students call Shyanne names?
2. What ideas did Mr. Brown, the school counselor, have for Shyanne to help her not be so shy?
3. How can you tell if someone is shy?
4. What are some ways you could help a friend overcome their shyness?

Extension Activities
■ Use the handout to help students come up with ideas for ways they could make a new student feel welcome in their school. Have the students share their list.

- When there are new students to your school, ask the counselor to have a friendship group so the new student will get to know some of the children in his/her class.

- Pair new students with a buddy student who will sit by them at lunch, help them find the necessary materials for class, play with them at recess, be there to answer any questions they may have, etc.

[Ways I Can Help a New Student Feel Welcome in our Class/School]

List all the things you can do to make a new student feel welcome at your school.

_____

_____

_____

_____

_____

_____

New Kid on the Block

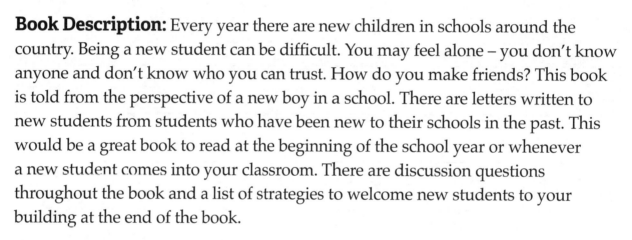

Book: *New Kid on the Block* by Jodi Baldwin

Publisher: Youthlight Inc.

Grade Levels: K-5

Book Description: Every year there are new children in schools around the country. Being a new student can be difficult. You may feel alone – you don't know anyone and don't know who you can trust. How do you make friends? This book is told from the perspective of a new boy in a school. There are letters written to new students from students who have been new to their schools in the past. This would be a great book to read at the beginning of the school year or whenever a new student comes into your classroom. There are discussion questions throughout the book and a list of strategies to welcome new students to your building at the end of the book.

Materials Needed:
■ Handout – Interview sheet

Preparation: None

Introduction: Have you ever been the new student at school? How did you feel? Did you worry about anything? How did you make friends? Today we are going to read a story about a boy who is new to the school. Listen for the ways he learned to make new friends.

Follow up Questions

1. How did the boy feel?

2. What were some things he worried about?

3. How did he make friends?

4. What advice did the students who wrote letters give to new students?

5. What could you do to make a new student feel more comfortable in our school?

Extension Activities

■ At the beginning of each school year, take pictures of the new students and put their picture up on a bulletin board near the main office so all the students can get to know who the new students are. Be sure to put the name of their classroom next to their picture, along with their name and something they like, a pet they have, or where they moved from.

■ Buddy the new students up with another student in their classroom so they have someone to play with at recess, to eat lunch with and to ask questions.

■ Have the new students be star student of the class early in the year so students can get to know them.

■ Talk with students in your class about how you can make new students feel welcome to your school no matter what time of year they come into the school.

■ At the beginning of the year, have students in class pair up and interview each other. Then have them introduce the other person to the entire class.

■ Do the Interview Activity and make it into a newspaper you can share with all classes in the grade level or even with the whole school.

Activity #19

[Interview a Student in Your Class]

What are things you have in common? What is something new you discovered?

My friend's name is _____

Things they like to do _____

_____

Favorite food _____

Favorite color _____

Favorite TV show _____

Favorite movie _____

Sports they enjoy _____

A good book they have read is _____

People in their family _____

Pets they have _____

Where they live _____

What they did over the summer _____

What they look for in a friend _____

_____

Board games they like to play _____

_____

Miranda: How Do I Stand in Your Shoes?

Book: *How Do I Stand in Your Shoes?* By Susan DeBell

Publisher: Youthlight Inc.

Grade Levels: 2-5

Book Description: Miranda's parents often tell her she is the best. This leads Miranda to be impatient with her classmates and even her teacher when they don't catch on to things as quickly as she does. She is mean to her classmates. Miranda calls them names and makes fun of them. Her teacher tells her she needs to stand in someone else's shoes. Miranda takes her literally and tries standing in different people's shoes. She doesn't get it so she asks her neighbor what it means to stand in someone else's shoes. Her neighbor explains empathy to her. Miranda imagines herself in the shoes of kids she has made fun of and realizes how badly they must feel. Miranda finally gets it! There are discussion questions and activities at the end of the story.

Materials Needed: None

Preparation: None

Introduction: Introduce Miranda Peabody – a girl who is the best at everything. Do you know anyone who is the best at everything? What is patience? Listen in the story to find out why Miranda loses her patience and how she learns to have more patience and understanding for others.

Follow up Questions

1. What caused Miranda to lose patience with everyone?

2. Have you ever lost your patience with someone? Tell when.

3. How does Miranda learn to have more patience and understanding for others?

4. What is empathy? How can you put yourself in someone else's shoes?

Extension Activities

■ In your journal, share a time when you showed empathy to someone else. How did that person feel? How did you feel?

■ In your journal, write about how empathy relates to being a person of character.

Gossiping

What is gossiping? Remember playing Telephone when you were a child? Students hear things about other students and pass it along in just the same way. Gossip can be hurtful and a way to bully others. Children need to learn how to stop gossiping. The books in this section teach children the importance of getting to know others and not "judging a book by its cover."

Miranda Peabody and the Case of the Lunchroom Spy

Book: *Miranda Peabody and the Case of the Lunchroom Spy* by Susan DeBell

Publisher: Youthlight Inc.

Grade Levels: PK-4

Book Description: Miranda Peabody is a talented writer. A girl in her class brings a notebook to lunch everyday. The rumor spreads that she is a spy. The girl is said to write down everything that is said and done in the lunchroom and on the playground. Then the girl reports to their teacher and the principal. The students are determined to stop her. Miranda writes a report about the girl's spying activities and she and her friends give a copy to everyone. No one will sit by the girl at lunch or play with her at recess. Meanwhile the teachers come up with a plan. Miranda and the girl are paired and have to talk with each other. Miranda realizes this girl has a great talent and is really a wonderful person. Someone she would like as a friend. The book has discussion questions and activities included.

Materials Needed:
- Friendship Handout

Preparation: None

Introduction: This would be a good story for the beginning of the school year or anytime a new student is coming into your classroom. Start by asking the students how they make friends. Then ask if they have ever decided they don't like someone. Tell them you are going to read a story about a girl who some students didn't like because they thought she was telling the teacher and principal on them. Ask them to listen to find out if the students were right and Marysara really is spying on them.

Follow up questions:

1. What made the students think Marysara was a spy?

2. Miranda knew that it was wrong to say and write mean things about other people. Why did she do it even when she knew it was wrong?

3. What did Miranda learn about Marysara when she had to meet her?

4. What did the other students think when they found out?

5. What consequence did the students who were mean to Marysara have?

6. Have you ever decided you didn't like someone just by the way they looked? Dressed? Acted?

Extension Activities

■ Have your students do the same activity that Miranda and her friends did at the second grade meeting. Have the students create a list of questions that they would ask when making a new friend. Match each student up with another student and have them ask their questions. Each day match up two new students until everyone in your class has had the chance to talk one-on-one with every student in the class.

■ Using the Friendship handout, make a list of characteristics you would like in a friend. See how many of the students you know meet the characteristics you listed for your friend. Then make a list of ways you can be a friend to others.

[Friendship]

Describe what you look for in a friend. Then list ways you can be a friend to others.

Characteristics I would like in a Friend	Ways I Can Be a Friend to Others

She Said WHAT About Me?

Book: *She Said WHAT About Me?* by Karen Dean

Publisher: Youthlight Inc.

Grade Levels: K-5

Book Description: A girl is very upset because her friend is spreading rumors about her and others are talking behind her back. She has many different feelings about it. She doesn't want to go to school. Her sister overhears her crying and tells her parents. She finally talks with her parents about what is happening. Her parents suggest she talk to the school counselor who give her ideas about how to handle the situation. She stands up for herself and feels much better. There are some questions and an activity at the end of the book.

Materials Needed:
- Handout, My Plan to STOP Rumors/Gossip

Preparation: None

Introduction: Ask students if they have ever heard someone gossiping or spreading rumors about others? Ask, "Are rumors true?" Tell them you are going to read a story about a girl whose friend is spreading rumors about her and others are gossiping behind her back. Ask them to listen to find out how she solves the problem.

Follow up questions
1. What happens in the story?
2. How does she feel when her friend is spreading rumors about her?
3. What is the difference between rumors and gossip?
4. How did she stand up for herself?
5. How can we stop rumors/gossip in our school?

Extension Activities
- Discuss with students ways that bullying/gossip could be stopped. Put these ideas on the board. Then have students complete the handout, My Plan to STOP Rumors/Gossip.

[My Plan to STOP Rumors/Gossip]

If someone spread a rumor or shared gossip with another student what you say or do?

How would you stop rumors at your school?

_____

_____

_____

_____

_____

The Drama Llama

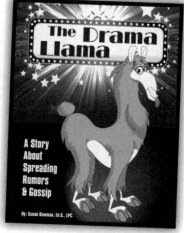

Book: *The Drama Llama* by Susan Bowman

Publisher: Youthlight Inc.

Grade Levels: 2-5

Book Description: This is a story about a llama who tries to become more popular by stirring up drama when the other animals were around. She did this by spreading rumors and gossip to the other animals. She learns that doing this does not make her more popular but instead causes the other animals to not want to be around her. It's a story about how stirring up drama with your friends does not help you gain more friends but can cause you to lose the friends you have.

Materials Needed:
■ Llama puppet (optional)

Preparation: None

Introduction: Ask students if they ever knew someone who liked to talk about other friends when they were not around. Ask, "What is a rumor?" Ask students how it feels to know someone is talking bad about you.

Follow up questions
1. What was the reason that the Drama Llama like to spread rumors?

2. What happened when she started adding others into the story?

3. How did the other animals act towards Drama Llama?

4. What happened when they stopped talking to Drama Llama?

5. How did the other animals feel when Drama Llama was all alone?

6. What did they do to make Drama Llama their friend again?

Extension Activities

■ Have students brainstorm different ways they could stop rumors or gossip from spreading.

■ Have students complete one of the follow up activities from the book.

Stop The Drama

For each situation give two examples of what you would do to stop the drama for spreading.

1. Your friend is very mad because she heard that you didn't like her.

2. Several students are saying mean things about a person you know.

3. Your friend just found out he failed a test and is so upset he kicks a chair.

4. Your friend is yelling at another student who said they didn't want to play with them.

6. You are asked to take out the trash and you start yelling that you're in the middle of a game.

Grief and Loss

The loss of a pet, moving, divorce or death of a beloved grandparent can cause one to experience grief and a sense of loss. Loss is a part of the life cycle. Children need to understand the feelings they have and how to cope with their loss. Sometimes it is hard for children to put into words how they feel. Is it okay to cry when you are sad? What is a casket? What is a wake? What is a funeral? What does it mean to die? These are all questions children might wonder but be afraid to ask. Bibliotherapy provides a way to address these issues using the stories to aid in the discussion.

Grief and loss are things children will continue to experience throughout their lives. It is important to explain these concepts in age appropriate terms so the child will understand. The books in this section provide real life examples of loss and strategies for children to use to get through their grief in terms they can understand.

A Rainbow of Hope

Book: *A Rainbow of Hope* by Linda Hagler

Publisher: Youthlight Inc.

Grade Levels: K-5

Setting: Small group, individual, parents

Book Description: This is a series of books on grief. Each story talks about a different situation in which grief may occur – moving, loss of a pet, death of a friend, death of a parent, adoption, fire and loss or house and property, new baby, divorce, dealing with bullies, and foster care. They are more appropriate for small groups and individual counseling than for use in the classroom due to the nature of the topics. Parents could use some of these books at home to initiate discussion. There is a leader's guide and ten story books – a book for each of the situations listed above. At the end of the story books are a list of questions for discussion. The leader's guide provides objectives for the lesson, an overview of the book, discussion questions and suggested activities for each story.

Materials Needed : None

Preparation: None

Introduction: In small groups or individual counseling, choose the book that best fits the situation and read it to the students. Ask the discussion questions in the leader's guide or make them more personal to fit the student's particular situation.

Follow up Questions

For the follow up questions, I would recommend using the ones in the leaders guide or personalizing them to each individual situation you are working with.

Extension Activities

Again, since there are so many various topics, I would recommend choosing one or several of the situations at the end of each story to use. There are ten to twenty activities listed for each lesson.

Good Grief

Book: *Good Grief* by Kim "Tip" Frank

Publisher: Youthlight Inc.

Grade Levels: 2-6

Setting: Small group, individual, parents

Book Description: There are two parts to this book. The first part, Good Grief: Understand Grief and Change helps children understand the grieving process. There are two or three questions after each page of the story. You can choose which questions are appropriate for the situation and children you are working with. The second part, William's Great Loss, is the story of a child going through the grieving process after losing his grandfather. There are discussion questions throughout the story. At the end of the book are activities that can be used to reinforce the concepts learned.

Materials Needed: None

Preparation: None

Introduction: In small group or individual counseling, use this book to move at your own pace with the child(ren) you are working with. Tell them loss is natural. Have them share what they lost. Tell them you are going to teach them about grief by reading a book together.

Follow up Questions

1. What did you learn about grief?

2. What are the five stages of grief? Did or are you experiencing any of these stages? Have them explain their answers.

3. What did it mean that the closer you are to the person who died the stronger the feelings of grief?

4. Does everyone grieve in the same way?

5. How can you help someone else who is experiencing a loss?

Extension Activities

■ Have grief groups where you can utilize students who have experienced grief in the past to help the students currently experiencing the grief (divorce groups, students who have moved, loss of pets, etc.)

■ Make a memory book of favorite memories the student had with the person who died. Have them draw pictures of favorite activities with that person and either they or you can type a story that goes with the picture. Then laminate the pages and bind them all into a book that the child can take home.

"Mommy What's Died?"

Book: *"Mommy, What's 'Died'?"* by Linda Swain Gill

Publisher: Youthlight Inc.

Grade Levels: PK-4

Setting: Classroom, small group, individual, parents

Book Description: This book describe what death is, what a casket and funeral are in a way young children can understand – through analogies. It is the story of a little boy who loses his grandfather and tries to make sense of things he hears the adults saying and doing. Finally he asks his mother what died is and this tale is told. This book can be used in large or small group, individual sessions or by parents.

Materials Needed:
- Handout on someone or a pet I know who has died

Preparation: None

Introduction: Has anyone ever lost something or someone? How did you feel? Today we will read the book, Mommy, What's 'Died'? The story will help you to understand some of the words adults use when someone has died and may answer some of the questions you have about what happens when someone dies.

Follow up Questions
1. What does it mean when someone dies? Where do they go?
2. What is a wake service? A casket? A funeral? Have you ever been to or seen any of these?
3. Why do people laugh and cry at funerals and wakes?
4. How can we keep the memory of someone we love who has died alive?

Extension Activities
- Be sure to reinforce the idea that death is a part of life. Sometimes talking about how a flower comes out in the spring, flowers in the summer, wilts in the fall and dies in the winter helps children to understand it as natural part of the life cycle.

Draw a picture of someone you know who has died. Or you may draw a picture of a pet who has died.

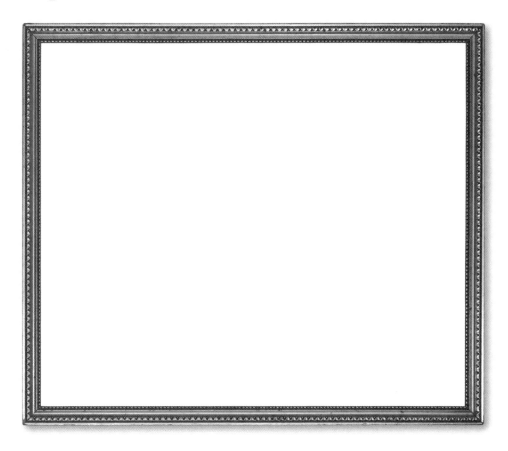

What did you like about this person or pet?

_____

_____

What are some favorite memories?

_____

_____

Internet Safety/ Personal Safety

Parenting today can be more challenging due to issues associated with cyber safety. Children have access to all types of material on the Internet. They may search for information for a report on a perfectly innocent sounding sight and may come across very inappropriate information. Children can instant message one another and may feel more comfortable saying things in an IM they wouldn't say face to face. There is also the risk of on-line predators who pretend to be a peer. How do we help children learn to navigate the Internet safely? How can we help them to learn safe sites and what to do when they encounter a sight that is not safe, or encounter bullying on-line? How do we teach them computer etiquette? The books in this section help students to learn to navigate the Internet safely, and learn what to do in dangerous situations.

Browser the Mouse

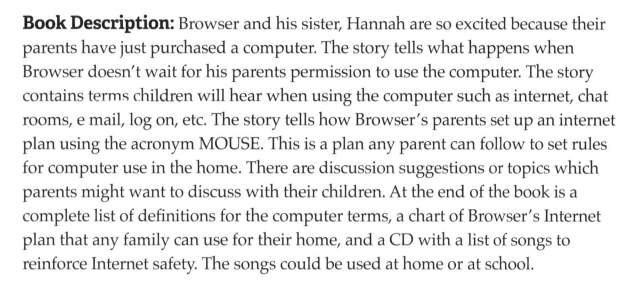

Book: *Browser the Mouse* by Barbara C. Trolley, Constance Hanel, Linda L. Shields

Publisher: Youthlight Inc.

Grade Levels: K-5

Book Description: Browser and his sister, Hannah are so excited because their parents have just purchased a computer. The story tells what happens when Browser doesn't wait for his parents permission to use the computer. The story contains terms children will hear when using the computer such as internet, chat rooms, e mail, log on, etc. The story tells how Browser's parents set up an internet plan using the acronym MOUSE. This is a plan any parent can follow to set rules for computer use in the home. There are discussion suggestions or topics which parents might want to discuss with their children. At the end of the book is a complete list of definitions for the computer terms, a chart of Browser's Internet plan that any family can use for their home, and a CD with a list of songs to reinforce Internet safety. The songs could be used at home or at school.

Materials Needed:
- Cardboard/construction paper for Class Internet Plan
- Handout – Letter to Parents
- Copy of Browser's Home Internet Plan for each student
- Handout – Class Internet Plan

Preparation: None

Introduction: Whenever you allow children at home or at school to begin using the computer it is an important time to introduce Brower the Mouse. Ask the children to raise their hands if they are already using the computer. Ask them how they learned to log on and what sites to use. Tell them you are going to read a story about a family who gets a new computer. Ask them to listen for what happens when Browser goes on the computer without his parent's permission.

Follow up Questions

1. What happened when Browser went on the computer without his parents permission?

2. What were some sites that Browser went to that were not safe?

3. Did it take courage for Browser to be honest with his parents? What does courage mean to you?

4. What is a pop up? What do you need to do if you are on the computer and a pop up comes on the screen?

5. Do you remember what MOUSE stands for? Discuss each letter of the acronym.

6. Do you have rules or an Internet Plan at your house? What are your family's rules about Internet use?

Extension Activities

■ Write an Internet Plan for the classroom in small groups. Have each group present their ideas. Take the common ideas and put them into one plan. Add or take out anything the class does not agree needs to be in the plan. When all have agreed, post the Internet Plan by the computers in the classroom and in the computer lab.

■ Have the students write a letter to their parents about the importance of having an Internet Plan. Give each student copies of the plan at the back of the book. Have them make any changes or additions they feel would work in their homes. Send a note home asking for feedback from parents on the activity.

■ Give parents a copy of your classroom Internet Plan.

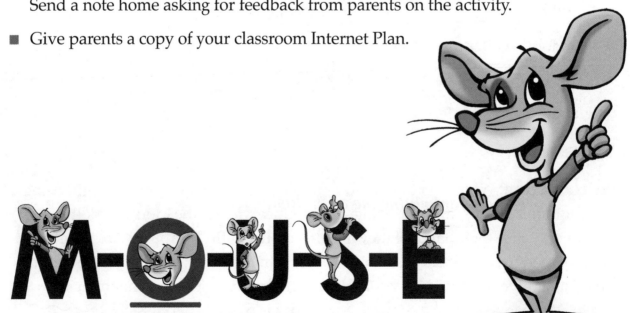

Activity #23

[Note for parents from students about importance of a home Internet plan]

Dear _____ ,

Today in class we read the book, Browser the Mouse.

It is a story about _____

_____

_____

_____

_____ .

It is important for us to have an Internet Plan at home. I have some ideas we might think about so we can be safe on the computer at home. My ideas are _____

_____

_____

_____ .

Thanks for helping me with this!

Love,

Activity #24

[Home Internet Plan]

Here is our home Internet Plan:

I _____ *promise to:*

_____

_____

_____

_____

_____

_____

_____.

X_____

Activity #25

[Classroom Internet Plan]

Dear Parents,

We wrote a classroom Internet Plan so we can be safe when working on the computers in our classroom.

This is our Plan: _____

_____

_____

_____

_____

_____

_____

_____

_____

_____ .

Be Safe, Jane, Be Safe

Book: *Be Safe, Jane, Be Safe* by Linda Hagler

Publisher: Youthlight Inc.

Grade Levels: K-5

Book Description: This book tells children about various situations that they need to be aware of to keep themselves safe such as on the playground, while riding their bike, walking on the sidewalk, etc. Knowing how to handle a situation can keep a child safe and help them to feel more secure. You could read parts of this book each day or the entire book in one session. There are activities at the end of the book to reinforce the various safety procedures.

Materials Needed:

- Handout – Adults I Can go to if I Feel Unsafe

- Handout – What to Do When

Preparation: None

Introduction: Tell students you are going to read a book about ways to stay safe in different situations. For younger students I would recommend reading parts of this book each day. There are so many different situations and safety rules that it will help them to remember the different rules if they are discussed and reinforced separately. For grades 3-5, this can be read in one sitting. Ask them to listen for the skill you are reading that day to find out what the safe thing to do is.

Follow up Questions

1. What is an emergency? What number can you call for help in an emergency?

2. Who is a stranger? What can you do if a stranger comes up to you and asks you for help? Offers you candy? Wants to help you?

3. What are some safety rules to remember on the playground? At the park?

4. What should you do if you get lost in a store?

5. What are the dangers of lighters/matches?

6. Name some safety rules for riding a bike?

7. What should you do if someone tries to touch the private parts of your body?

8. What are some rules to remember when using the Internet?

Extension Activities

- Have students list trusted adults they could go to if they don't feel safe. Use the handout.

- Have students create a list of safety rules for the playground. Put the rules on a poster and decorate it. Hang the posters up around school.

- Make a list of situations and what to do in those situations. Use the handout What to Do When.

Activity #26

[Adults I can go to if I Feel Unsafe]

Write the names of who you can go to for each situation:

Someone is bullying you on the school bus.

_____

_____

You see a bad picture on the computer.

_____

_____

A stranger approaches you after school and offers you a ride.

_____

_____

Another student pushes you in the hallway.

_____

_____

A friend tells you they want to hurt themself.

_____

_____

You know someone who is being abused at home.

_____

_____

You see someone with a weapon at school.

_____

_____

[What to Do When]

Write an answer for the safe thing to do for each situation.

➡ If there was a fire at my house I would _____

_____

➡ It's important to know my name, address and phone number in case I get lost or need to call for help.

     ☺ My name is _____

     ✉ My address is _____

     ☎ My phone number is _____

➡ If someone I don't know comes up and asks me to find their lost kitty, I would

_____

➡ If someone tries to touch me in my private area, I would_____

_____

➡ If I got lost at a store, I would _____

_____

➡ If I found a lighter, I would _____

_____

➡ Before I cross the street, I need to _____

_____

Self-Confidence and Motivation

Why do you do what you do? What motivates you to persevere even when things are difficult? As adults we deal with these questions. So do our children. Helping children understand what motivates them and how to persevere even when math or reading is difficult are important life skills to learn. At risk students may have a more difficult time finding someone to motivate them into making the right choices in life.

The books in this section help students to analyze their strengths and weaknesses, look for ways to maximize their strengths and ways to improve on their weaknesses. They provide strategies for believing in oneself and provide inspiring stories of other's successes or challenges and inspire children and teens to want to do their best.

Letters from Prison

Book: *Letters from Prison* by Monique Holeyfield

Publisher: Youthlight Inc.

Grade Levels: 6-12

Setting: small group, individual, parents

Book Description: Prisoners write letters directly to troubled teens in hopes of helping them avoid the path they took. The goal of the book is for teens to actually read the stories themselves. The men and women who wrote these letters did so voluntarily. They are written by people who speak about how they were troubled teens. After each letter there are discussion questions and a reflection section for students to journal their thoughts. At the end of the book is a list of recommended reading for parents and teenagers.

Materials Needed: None

Preparation: None

Introduction: Because this book would be better used in small group or individual counseling sessions, the introduction will depend on the child's background, home situation and school situation. Tell the student you have some stories to share from people who have been there.

Follow up Questions

1. Could you identify with the person writing the letter? What parts did you identify with? How do you feel about what they had to say?

2. Are there things in your life you are struggling with? Who can help you?

Extension Activities

■ Encourage the student to complete the reflections section in the book after the stories. What choices are they faced with? What options do they have?

■ If possible, form a small group with students from your school or students from area schools who have parents who are incarcerated.

■ Provide mentors for students who have been in trouble.

Every Child Has A Gift

Book: *Every Child Has A Gift* by Tom Carr

Publisher: Youthlight Inc.

Grade Levels: K-12

Setting: Classroom, small group, individual, parents

Book Description: How can we help children to become the best person they can be? Studies have shown that children who come from disadvantaged backgrounds can succeed with the help of at least one caring adult in their lives. There are many factors that impact children over which they have no control. Try to see past these factors and look at the child. The first part of the book addresses how you can be that caring adult. It covers how everyone wants to be good at something, our heroes, the gifts that each of us possess, how to succeed and the secret of life. The second part of the book contains stories that motivate one to be the best they can be and tells how others succeeded despite difficulties in their lives. The stories could be read over the daily morning announcements, used in class or with individuals and small groups. Parents could read these inspirational messages with their children. This book has strategies, suggestions and stories for helping kids make the most of their "raw material."

Materials Needed:
- Handout My Hero
- Handout Self-evaluation

Preparation: None

Introduction: Have you ever felt like you couldn't do anything right? Why try anyway? Everyone wants to be good at something. Over the next few weeks we will be talking about how to be successful, our heroes, our passions and who can help us be successful. Today we are going to read about the formula for success.

Follow up Questions

1. What is the formula for success?

2. Do you believe that you can be successful?

3. What are some things you are passionate about?

4. Who can help you to be successful?

Extension Activities

■ Have children research some of the people listed in the book. Have them report on the person's gifts, talents, and occupation. Have them tell what personal strengths they had which helped them to succeed.

■ Use the handout and have the children write about their hero. Why did they choose this person as their hero? What personal strengths does this person have that you admire? What character traits do they demonstrate? Write about this person's life. Did they overcome any adversities? Have the children share their heroes with the class.

■ Use the Handout to have the students look at their strengths (what they do well) and their weaknesses (what they need to work on). Have them write a goal about how they will improve on one of their weaknesses. Make sure they include the steps they will take to achieve the goal – what will they need to do? How often/long will they do it? When will they do it? Where will they do it?

■ One of the secrets of life is to serve others. Have a discussion with your class about ways they personally could serve others, ways your class could serve others and then ways your school could serve others. Choose one of the ways your class could serve others and do it.

Read Tom Carr's other book of inspirational stories called *Changing Young Lives: One Story at a Time* available through YouthLight.

Activity #28

[My Hero]

Write about your hero. Include things such as: Why you chose this person as your hero? What personal strengths does this person have that you admire? What character traits do they demonstrate? Write about this person's life. Did they overcome any adversities? Share your hero with the class.

My Hero/Heroine is _____

The reason(s) I admire to this person is because: _____

_____

_____

_____

_____

_____

Why I chose this person? _____

_____

_____

_____

_____

_____

Activity #29

[Self-Evaluation]

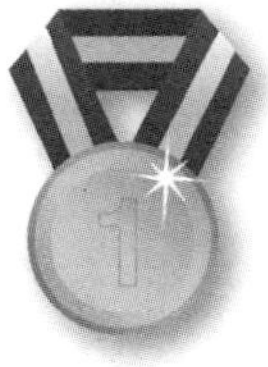

Things I do Well:

____

____

____

____

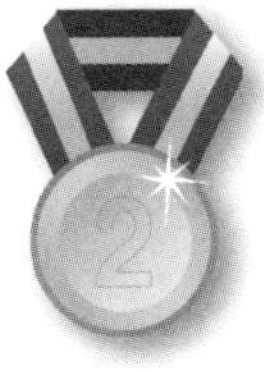

Things I need to work on:

____

____

____

____

Things I am passionate about ____________________________

____

____

____

Write a goal for one of the things you need to work on. Be sure to include the steps it will take to achieve the goal. What will you do? How often/long will you do it? When will you do it? Where will you do it?

____

____

____

____

____

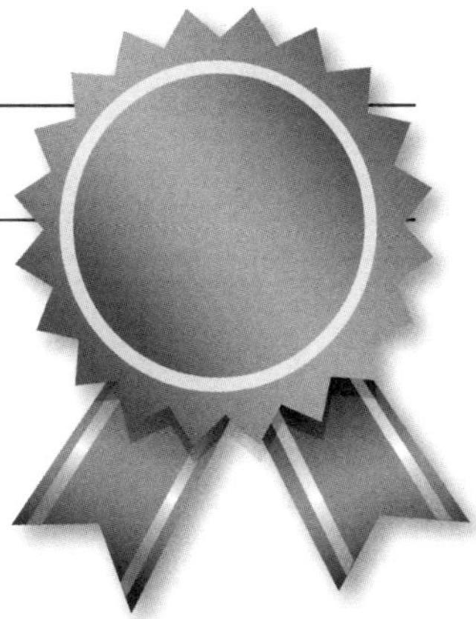

Stretch, the Long-Necked Rabbit

Book: *Stretch, the Long-Necked Rabbit* by Robert P. Bowman

Publisher: Youthlight Inc.

Grade Levels: K-5

Book Description: Stretch is a long-necked rabbit who looks different from the other rabbits. He is unhappy that his neck is too long so he goes to the barber to get a "hare cut" for his neck. After three tries, his neck looks like all the other rabbits and Stretch is very happy. The next day, he is sad again because he can no longer reach the highest berries on the bush, watch for predators and warn the other animals, and see things that are up high. He tries to stretch his neck back to the original size but nothing works. This is a good story for accepting your own differences, the differences of others, talking about how students can "stretch" themselves and do better in their weaker areas or for career development.

Materials Needed:

- Copy of Stretch using the master in the book

- Rubber cement

- Cornstarch

- Scissors

Preparation: Xerox enough copies of Stretch so each student will have one. Cover back with rubber cement and let it dry. Then cover with cornstarch.

Introduction: Ask students what the world would be like if we all looked, talked and dressed the same. Would you want to live in a world like that? Stretch is a long-necked rabbit who wants badly to be the same as every other rabbit. As we read the story, listen to find out if stretch is able to change his neck to be like the other rabbits (follow directions from book for how to cut the neck).

Follow up Questions

1. Was Stretch able to make his neck look like all the other rabbits?

2. How did he do it?

3. Was he happy after his neck looked like the other rabbits? Why not?

4. Sometimes there are good things about the ways we are different from each other. Can you think of a way you are different from others? Is there something good about that difference?

Extension Activities

■ Ask all the students to come sit in a circle. Ask all the students wearing white socks to stand. Have them look at who is standing. Then have everyone sit. Ask students with pockets on their clothes to stand. Again have them look at who is standing. Repeat this many times using whatever criteria you would like. At the end, ask them if they are all alike. Then ask if they are all different. "Is it okay to be different?" "Why/why not?" Then relate to Stretch and how being different provided safety for the other rabbits and food for him.

■ Have students draw how they are alike and different. Let them share their pictures with each other.

■ Have students make their own Stretch. Then have them decide whether to keep his long neck or shorten it. Have them share which neck they chose for Stretch and why.

Secrets to Success

What does it take to be a successful student? Study skills need to be taught so students know how and when to study. Effort, paying attention, perseverance, learning to work together, good attitude, asking for help and following directions are all skills involved in being a successful student. Students need to know what these skills are and why they are important. Twenty-first century skills focus on these areas as they are also skills to help one be successful in the work place.

The books in this section covers these skills at K-1, 2-3 and 4-5. The stories are ones the students will easily identify with. The characters and the messages are clear.

How Grinner Became a Winner

Book: *How Grinner Became a Winner*
by Robert P. Bowman and John N. Chanaca

Publisher: Youthlight Inc.

Grade Levels: K-5

Book Description:
Grinner is a flying squirrel who believes he can't learn to fly. He gets so angry he runs off into the woods where he meets Blackbelt, a raccoon. Blackbelt teaches Grinner five steps to become a winner. Each step has a separate story to reinforce the concepts to be learned. After each step, Grinner receives a different color wristband from Blackbelt.

Materials Needed:
- Handout "I Can" statements or empty can to make your own "I CAN"
- Handout on Making an Effort
- Handout on Character Traits needed to show effort

Preparation: None

Introduction: Ask the students if they know what a flying squirrel is. Say the main character in our story today is a flying squirrel who believes he cannot fly. Please listen to find out how Grinner learns he can fly and how to be a winner.

Follow up Questions
1. Why was Grinner convinced he couldn't fly?
2. What happened in the story to change Grinner's feelings about flying?
3. What is the first step to being a winner?
4. How did Grinner learn to show he was a winner?

5. What does it mean to start like a winner? Have you ever had to do something that you didn't want to do? Did you keep putting off doing it?

6. Did Grinner finish like a winner? What does it mean to finish like a winner?

Extension Activities

■ Have students make a list of things they can do using the I Can sheet. Be sure the list includes skills from many areas of life such as academic, social, personal, etc.

■ Have the students define effort. Ask them what they need to put the most effort into at school. At home.

■ Have students list the character traits one needs to give their best effort.

I CAN!

 Write all the things you "Can" do well:

_____

_____

_____

_____

_____

I feel _____ **when I see how many things...**

I CAN DO!

Activity #31

[Making an Effort]

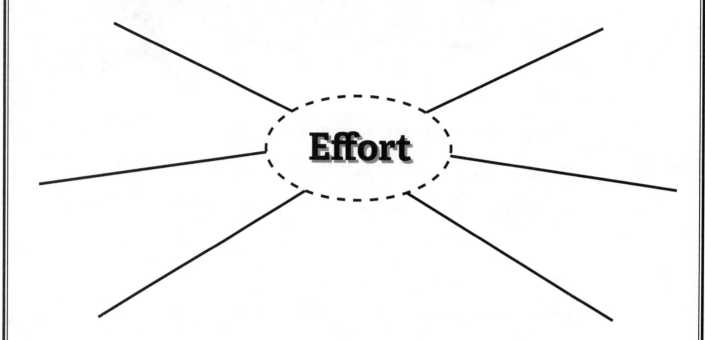

Effort

What I need to Put Effort into at:

School:

Home:

What is the definition of "Effort?"

[Character Traits]

The character traits I need to give my best effort

_____

_____

_____

The character traits I show every day

_____

_____

_____

The character traits I need to work on

_____

_____

_____

Write a goal to improve on one character trait – be sure to include the
"effort" you will need to achieve this goal.

The Super Student Program

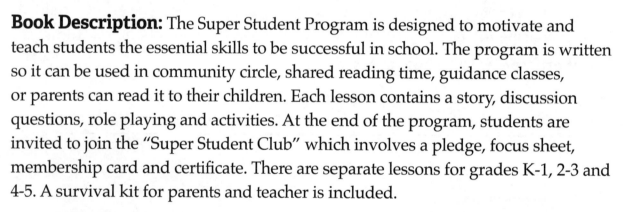

Book: *The Super Student Program* by John Chanaca

Publisher: Youthlight Inc.

Grade Levels: K-5

Setting: Classroom, small group, individual, parents

Book Description: The Super Student Program is designed to motivate and teach students the essential skills to be successful in school. The program is written so it can be used in community circle, shared reading time, guidance classes, or parents can read it to their children. Each lesson contains a story, discussion questions, role playing and activities. At the end of the program, students are invited to join the "Super Student Club" which involves a pledge, focus sheet, membership card and certificate. There are separate lessons for grades K-1, 2-3 and 4-5. A survival kit for parents and teacher is included.

Materials Needed:
■ Handout Effort/My Goal Sheet

Preparation: None

Introduction: This year I would like everyone in the class to be successful and feel empowered as learners. To accomplish this, we are going to participate in the Super Student program. This will teach you the skills to be a successful student. I am so excited to introduce you to this program. At the end of the lessons, you will be invited to join the Super Student Club. Let's get started.

Follow up Questions
1. What skills does a super student need?

2. Do you feel you understand each of these skills? Are you ready to put the effort in to use these skills everyday?

3. Being a super student often means trying even when you don't feel like it. Can

you motivate yourself to keep trying even when you don't feel like it? What are some ways each of us can motivate ourselves to keep trying?

Extension Activities

- Have students write positive affirmations to themselves on a 3 x 5 card so that they can refer to it to motivate themselves when they need that extra push. Teach students statements such as "Try and push yourself," "I CAN do this," etc.

- Talk about effort with your class. Ask them to list things they need to put effort into at school. Tell them in order to reach our goals it is the effort that counts. Have them write a goal that includes the effort needed to reach the goal. The effort should include what will I need to do, when will I do it, for how long, and where. For example – I want to know my addition fact. The effort would be practicing my facts for 10 minutes every day right after school. Use the accompanying handout.

Activity #33

[My Goal Sheet + EFFORT]

The goal I need to work on:

_____

The effort it will take to reach my goal:

What will I need to do? _____

How long will I need to do this? _____

When will I do it? _____

Where will I do it? _____

Tally the days you put the effort toward your goal:

Did you reach your goal? Why or why not?

Out of This World – Max Strives for Success

Book: *Out of This World: Victory Through Motivation*
by Jon Filliti & Eric Erbes

Publisher: Youthlight Inc.

Grade Levels: 5-8

Book Description: The final segment of this series finds Max feeling responsible for them not knowing where Tiglos is. In the last segment Tiglos has sent a signal to show where he is located and Max was goofing around and missed the signal. He can sit there feeling sorry for himself or he can try to do something to find Tiglos. Max learns that motivation and perseverance help him to figure out difficult problems such as where Tiglos is located. The book contains activities to teach motivation and effort.

Materials Needed:

■ Handout on Personal Strengths

■ Handout What Motivates Me

Preparation: Set up an anger control station in your classroom.

Introduction: Ask students if they ever get frustrated and give up. Tell them you are going to read a story about a boy who made a mistake. He is feeling sorry for himself and is ready to give up. Then the boy finds a way to motivate himself to try to find an answer and to keep trying even when it is hard.

Follow up Questions

1. Why won't Marlania let Max help find Tiglos?

2. What motivated Max to stop feeling sorry for himself?

3. What was one of Max's strengths? Did his strength help them find Tiglos?

4. What is persistence?

5. Have you ever made a mistake? Did you give up or use your strengths to help you figure out the answer?

6. Name some things that motivate you to keep trying even when something is difficult.

Extension Activities

- Have students complete the handout, My Personal Strengths.

- Have students journal about why it is important to keep trying and not give up when something is difficult.

- Ask students if someone can be motivated by something other than money. Have them write what motivates them on the Motivation handout.

[My Personal Strengths]

Draw a picture of 4 of your personal strengths below.

Activity #33

[What Motivates Me]

Name what motivates you to do the following:

Schoolwork _____

Follow Rules _____

Do your chores _____

Complete homework _____

Get along with others _____

Keep clean _____

Obey parents _____

Appendix
Books with Multiple Guidance Topics

The books in this section contain stories with multiple topics. Some are a compilation of short stories which can be used once a day or when you are covering the topic in class. Some contain stories about the same character covering different topics.

The Adventures of Dakota

Book: *The Adventures of Dakota* by Susan Bowman

Publisher: Youthlight Inc.

Grade Levels: K-5

Setting: Classroom or small group

Book Description: This book contains eight stories each with different topics of focus. The topics include rumors, bullying, diversity, personal strengths, grief and loss, conflict resolution, prejudice and conquering fears. Each story has "Paws Time" where you stop the story and children get into groups or packs and brainstorm how Dakota can solve the problem. They report their answers back to the class. Then the story continues. At the end of the story there are follow up questions and activities for the students. Since the topics are different, you can read the stories any time you think appropriate or you can read them one per day.

Materials Needed:
- Copies of the Wolf Paw Print from the book

Preparation: None

Introduction: Ask students, "What is a reputation"? Can a reputation be good or bad? How does someone get a "reputation?" Today we are going to read a book that begins with Dakota, a wolf that has a bad reputation. Listen for how Dakota gets his reputation and if it is a good or bad reputation.

Follow up Questions
For the follow up questions, I would recommend using the ones in the story since the "Paws Time" questions are very applicable and provide the students the opportunity to participate in the story. The follow up questions are well written and applicable as well.

Cut out copies of the Paw Print from the book and divide the students into small groups or "packs" and have each group chose a name for their pack.

1. What does "kill them with kindness "mean?

2. When does this happen in the story?

3. Would this be a good strategy to use when someone is mean to you or tries to bully you?

Extension Activities

■ Tell the students that you will be reading stories about Dakota throughout the year. You can keep them in the same groups for the stories or mix the groups up as the year goes on. There are suggestions for composition of the pack or groups in the book. Before you begin, have the students' research animals that move in groups or packs. Have them report back to the class what they discover about these animals and why they move in groups/packs.

■ Do people move in groups or packs? How? Talk about cliques, groups of friends, etc. Talk about how groups can promote good or bad behavior depending on the composition of the group. This can be related to bullying, stopping bullying with groups, organization which help others, etc. How do groups impact rumors? Bullying? Gossip? Helping others? Which type of group would you rather belong – harmful – gossiping, bullying, rumors or helpful – offering to play and sit by a new student at lunch, helping a group of younger students learn to read or with their math, picking up trash around the school or community?

■ What is body language? This is also called nonverbal communication. Talk with students about some common messages sent through nonverbal communication – hands on hips, rolling eyes, smiles, hand gestures, etc.

Return to the Land: The Search for Compassion

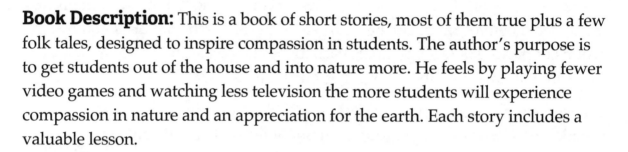

Book: *Return to the Land: The Search for Compassion* by Tom Carr

Publisher: Youthlight Inc.

Grade Levels: 3-12

Book Description: This is a book of short stories, most of them true plus a few folk tales, designed to inspire compassion in students. The author's purpose is to get students out of the house and into nature more. He feels by playing fewer video games and watching less television the more students will experience compassion in nature and an appreciation for the earth. Each story includes a valuable lesson.

Materials Needed: None

Preparation: None

Introduction: This book can be used in numerous ways. You can read a story a day, read a story that fits with a topic you are covering in class, have it as a resource for students, use it for guidance class, etc.

Follow up Questions

Since there are so many stories, you can devise your own questions for each. A question that could be asked of every story is, "What is the lesson to be learned in this story?"

Extension Activities

■ Every story is so different in setting and characters. You can have students journal about the topics, write stories showing the character trait displayed in the story, act out the stories, do further research on the topic, etc.

About the Author

Stef Weber has an M.A. in counseling and an M.A. in elementary administration. She has taught, counseled and coached students in grades PK-12 for the past thirty-five years. Stef has counseled high school students for eight years and elementary students for twenty-seven years. As an advocate for children, she continues to work daily to find ways to help children learn to help themselves and to help families. Stef has been an adjunct professor of psychology and education at Northeast Iowa Community College and Clarke College in Dubuque, Iowa for the past eighteen years. Stef is the coauthor of "Coming to School is Really Cool." Stef serves on the curriculum committee for the State of Iowa School Counselor Summit. In her spare time she loves dancing with her granddaughter, gardening, working out and sharing good times with friends. She is also a soon-to-be grandmother again.